You Can't Imagine

You Can't Imagine

A Mother Shares Her Daughter's Journey
with Traumatic Brain Injury

by Debbie Taylor

*A portion of the proceeds from this book will be donated
to Mothers Against Drunk Driving (MADD)
and the Brain Injury Association.*

Table of Contents

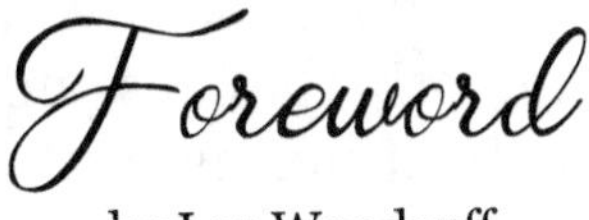

Foreword

by Lee Woodruff

In 2006, during his ninth reporting trip to Iraq, my journalist husband Bob was critically injured by a roadside bomb in Iraq. That phone call, from ABC News, changed the lives of our entire family in an instant. We suddenly joined the ranks of the millions of families who have had to navigate the often life changing affliction of a traumatic brain injury (TBI).

In the early days of Bobs injury, the 36 days of a medically induced coma, the multiple surgeries, uncertainty and fear, I operated day-to-day, sometimes even hour-to-hour. I came to rely heavily on the four "F"s in my life—or what I would call the four legs of my stool; faith, friendship, family and funny, a sense of humor being a critical component to get through difficult times.

When Bob awoke, very suddenly, we began our forward journey to heal. No longer in the limbo of a coma, we faced a greater challenge, the day to day hard work of rehabilitation and the two steps forward, one step back nature that Debbie Taylor's wonderful book depicts so accurately.

We came to understand that in addition to the tragic civilian injuries and accidents that happen each year, there were hundreds of thousands of young men and women returning from the wars in Iraq and Afghanistan with these injuries. There was a large spectrum, from the obvious head wounds like those Bob had suffered, to more hidden injuries such as mild traumatic brain injury, post traumatic stress, combat stress and depression, mental health issues that our country was not been prepared to deal with in such numbers.

TBI is one of the worst tragedies that can befall an

individual. It's the immediate nature of injury, the speed with which it permanently changes and upends lives and relationships that is so stunning. Unlike a slow burning diagnosis or another type of disease, there is a clear line between "before" and "after" which creates a sense of emotional whiplash.

Why is TBI so devastating? When the injured person is your loved one, there is a special element of heartbreak, an unusual tangle of emotions, sorrow and gratitude and so much uncertainty. There are no percentages to shoot for, no norms, no one can tell you exactly how much your loved one will recover or how much of "him" will return.

In that first year, lying beside my sleeping husband, he was there, but not there, physically present, but with pieces missing. It was as if his brain was an engine and someone had reached inside and fiddled with the wiring.

I've often said that we cannot rewind the tape of our lives. And I don't believe that "things happen for a reason." I don't believe God is up in heaven choosing who among us gets cancer or whose child is hit by a drunk driver. That doesn't mean it hurts any less, but its one step closer to moving past the inevitable "why me?"

For anyone or their loved ones navigating the journey of brain injury, it is a frightening, complex and often discouraging road. It's the expertise no one ever wants to gain, the club in which you never want to be a member. There are far too few beacons of information, hope, and realism.

"You Can't Imagine, A Mother's Memoir of Her Daughter's Journey with Traumatic Brain Injury" has just added one more beacon. Debbie shares her story with the hope of helping others.

The tale begins like any ordinary summer day. Blue sky. Two friends decide to skip school and head to the beach. They are a month away from graduation and for Debbie, she is about to experience the empty nest when her daughter Lexi heads off to college. Debbie herself had found love again after divorce, she was planning a wedding and looking forward to the rest of her life.

Lexi called her mother to tell her she and her friend were heading to the beach. If this were a movie, Debbie would be able to stop the tape here, rewind it, delay her daughter on that road trip or simply tell her she couldn't go. But life doesn't work that way. We don't get to re-do the thousands of small, incremental choices that determine the story of our lives.

"If only, if only, if only . . ." is such a familiar refrain for anyone who has experienced their own "in an instant" moment. But at a certain point, the only alternative to move forward is to set these repetitive thoughts aside and get to work with the long, messy, often agonizing business of recovery.

As a mother, that's exactly what Debbie did. She jumped in with both feet and this book is that story. It's a mother's story. It's a personal story, as all stories of brain injury are.

What Debbie has written is a step-by-step bird's eye view into this journey, from the moment she learns the news through the acute care and rehab worlds. It's a memoir, but it's also a practical guide, with helpful lists and information; things she wished she had known about the injury and care, advocacy, dealing with friends or disseminating information, preparing the home and so much more.

One of my favorite sections was the helpful lines of "self talk" which offers a variety of mantras to get through the dark times, when despair swamps the brain.

Debbie has written a book that not only illuminates the rollercoaster ride of TBI, but functions as a roadmap for others travelling along this horrible highway, pitted with both big heartbreaks and small, welcome miracles.

Lee Woodruff and her husband, Bob Woodruff, are the authors of *In an Instant: A Family's Journey of Love and Healing* (2007). Lee also authored *Perfectly Imperfect: A Life in Progress* (2009) as well as her novel, *Those We Love Most* (2012).

Introduction

Believe me, you never want to become an "expert" in any medical terminology. You never want to go through what my family has gone through since May 19, 2017. I knew about traumatic brain injuries from the brave soldiers who were injured in the wars and reading about football players' injuries. I even watched the movie "Concussion" starring Will Smith. *Little did I know how much I was soon to learn.*

I am sharing my story in the hope of helping others. I will never know why the crash happened to Abby and Lexi, but from the beginning, my goal was to help others—and have something positive come of it. That is the only way I could get through the early days, and it's something I continue to hold onto. This book is one part of that. I now have a support group for young people who have a brain injury and their families and caregivers. I also want to educate all drivers, but especially younger ones, about the consequences of driving impaired or distracted. Although we will never know if any lives have been saved, based on the stories I have already heard, I think it is highly likely.

The other reason I want to share my story is you see things like this on the news and think, my God, that poor family. You may see an occasional follow-up, but you never know what really happens. I always thought . . . here but for the grace of God go I. Well, now it was our turn. I lived every parent's worst nightmare, and it was a million times worse than you could even imagine. So many people would say to me, "I can't imagine what you are going through," and I would say, "No, you can't." Unless you have been through something similar, you simply cannot imagine. For those of you who have been down the road of trauma, I understand. I hope this book helps you, too. This is a club no one wants to belong to.

I believe Lexi survived for a reason—and that Abby is her guardian angel. I was not a particularly religious person before the crash, but now I pray often not only to God but also to Abby. Lexi's story is a work in progress but, as of now, I can tell you my story and what I have learned and what I hope will make it a little easier for another family to navigate through a trauma of any kind.

Every brain injury is unique, and there are lots of ways to experience trauma and many forms of it. I hope my words of wisdom help anyone who is on the hard road of recovering from trauma.

This is my story and told with the best of my recollections. Some of the names and places have been changed to protect the individuals' privacy.

According to the Center for Disease Control's web site (CDC.gov), "traumatic brain injury (TBI) is a major cause of death and disability in the United States. TBIs contribute to about 30 percent of all deaths. Every day, 153 people in the United States die from injuries that include TBI. Those who survive a TBI can face effects that last a few days, or the rest of their lives. Effects of TBI can include impaired thinking or memory, movement, sensation (e.g., vision or hearing), or emotional functioning (e.g., personality changes, depression). These issues not only affect individuals but can have lasting effects on families and communities."

Things You Never Want:

- To tell your son to make sure they do everything they can, so your daughter will survive.

- To be called "next of kin."

- To have everyone in the Burn Trauma ICU know you by sight, if not by name.

- To be the subject of pity.

- To have to talk to the fatal crash investigative team.

- To wait outside while they change your eighteen-year-old's diaper.

- To be in any critical care unit.

- To become a traumatic brain injury go-to person in your community.

- To have the lead fatal crash investigator, the prosecutor's office, and your attorney's office numbers in the contact list of your phone.

- To have to help your daughter decide on what tattoo she will get to memorialize her best friend who was killed in the same crash she survived.

Chapter 1

My Perfect New Life

"You're the best thing that ever happened to me."
– Gladys Knight

I grew up in Salt Lake City, Utah, then married and quickly moved to California where both our kids were born. In 1999, I had an opportunity to move to Virginia for my job. I had hoped moving would help our relationship, but it didn't. After twenty years of marriage, we decided to separate, and later we divorced. Lexi was one year old and Marshall was 10. I always said we made the best of a bad situation. My ex-husband was close to both of our kids while he lived in Virginia. When Lexi had started fifth grade, and Marshall was in tenth grade, he moved to Arizona to live with his mother.

It took a few years to adjust to living in Virginia, but I quickly acquired a wonderful group of friends and was very busy and socially active. In May 2017, Marshall was 27, had graduated from William and Mary in 2012, and was a certified public accountant (CPA). He lived locally, and we saw him often. My kids have always been extremely close and they are my proudest achievement. However, I was ready to have my own life, having been a mom for more than 27 years. I joked I would be doing the happy dance when Lexi graduated from high school and went off to college.

Back when my daughter was 13, I realized I could have

my own life, so I started dating for real. I dated a guy for six months, and we had plans for the weekend when he simply disappeared. I thought he was dead, but I learned he was fine—but he was not available to me.

I took a month or two to recover. During that time, I realized I wanted a significant other in my life, and now I had a mission. I joined every dating website and contacted lots of men. I approached it like a job hunt. On one dating site, I contacted an interesting guy, but then didn't hear from him for quite some time. Finally, he emailed me back and said to contact him on his personal email as he wasn't on that site any longer. We emailed back and forth and talked on the phone. Ray and I finally decided to meet.

We had two more dates, but I was also continuing my quest. When I didn't hear from him, I emailed, and he invited me to his house for a tailgating party and a college football game. A large group of friends were at his house for the tailgate, but we sat alone at the football game. When he walked me to my car, he finally kissed me. He also asked me to text him when I arrived home. That was it for me, and I cancelled my various dating sites. We agreed quickly to be exclusive to each other.

We took our time, but Ray became a huge part of my life. His son was at Virginia Tech, and was home only for holidays and during the summer. It was a few months before he met my kids, but gradually we became a family. We joked that I was everything he didn't want. He didn't want anyone with kids at home, and Lexi of course, still was. I was younger than he was, and he had never dated anyone younger. The only things I had going for me: I had a job, and was able to support myself, and I liked bowling, which I mentioned in my dating profile. The funny thing is we have been together seven years and have gone bowling only twice.

Originally, he told me he didn't want to get married,

and I said okay, that wasn't a deal breaker for me, but I also explained that I was the marrying type. It was funny that he couldn't even say the word "marriage" for a long time.

Ray's daughter and son-in-law moved to Japan a few weeks after we met. Ray and I took Lexi to Japan to see his daughter, Ellie, and her husband David, in 2013. That was a great bonding experience—nothing like being thousands of miles from home and not speaking the language to quickly learn how we worked together.

Over time Ray became a dad to Lexi as he was around at least a few days a week. He attended all her field hockey games and helped teach her to drive. He was at the pre-prom festivities to meet her date, whom he called by the wrong name.

Finally, in November 2016 he started to get his house ready to go on the market. The plan was he would sell it and move in with me about the time Lexi went off to college.

On December 31, 2016, I made the first dinner in his newly remodeled kitchen, and when we sat down to eat, he got down on one knee. I thought he dropped something. He asked me to marry him, and of course, I said yes. We both cried a bit. We had been talking about getting engaged for a while, and although he has great taste in jewelry, he agreed I could pick out my own ring. On January 2nd we were at a "big box store" right when they opened to look at rings, and when we walked around the jewelry case, we saw a sapphire ring we both liked. Finally, I could make the long-awaited announcement.

Lexi was ready to go away to college even before her senior year began. She was independent and ready to be an "adult." She had applied to 10 universities. I thought it was crazy to send in that many applications. She was accepted at her first choice, University of Santa Barbara—but I had to be the bad guy and tell her no. I told her I couldn't pay for out-of-state tuition, and I wouldn't let her graduate with a ton of debt. We live in Virginia, and we are blessed to have wonderful colleges and universities. At one point she was deciding between Virginia Tech and College of Charleston. In April, after we went to Virginia Tech's Hokie weekend, she finally decided to commit to Tech.

I was happy and relieved that Lexi had decided on a college. She was excited to go, and thrilled that her best friend, Abby, had also chosen Virginia Tech.

We spent the next month planning her graduation parties and getting ready for senior prom. When Marshall graduated from high school, we had only six people in our family, but now it was significantly larger with Ray's family added. My mom, sister, and niece were coming from Salt Lake City. They hadn't all been to Virginia since Marshall graduated from William and Mary in 2012. My best friend, Jamie, was coming from California with her boyfriend, and Ray's sister Olga was also coming with her husband, son, and his girlfriend. I was *so excited*. Graduation was scheduled for 7:30 p.m. on a Friday night in June, and we decided to have dinner for everyone at our house before the ceremony because we would have about 20 people in town. The weekend before graduation we had planned a party for family and friends. Lexi and I decided what food we would have, not only for her graduation party, but also for dinner the night of graduation. None of the parties happened.

Ray sold his house and officially moved in with me on May 5, with plans to get married sometime in 2018. We weren't in a hurry, but on May 9, he said I should start planning the wedding for the following summer. We had to choose a time when Lexi would be home from college, so we looked at early June 2018.

In addition to Ray moving in, and my youngest child soon graduating from high school and going away to college, I decided to change careers.

I had worked in the electronic security industry and truly was burned out. I went to a networking event at a local, top-notch entertainment center and ran into one of their event planners I knew. I asked if they were hiring. On their website, I found a job and applied. Because it was different from anything I had done, I didn't expect anything to happen. I received a call and completed a video interview. The following day I went in and met with the director of sales and the general manager. Soon after, I received a call offering me the job of sales manager in Virginia Beach. Before I accepted, I had to tell them about all the days I needed off for Lexi's graduation and taking her to college; they said that was okay. I would sell memberships to individuals and businesses, plan events, and socialize with members. It was my dream job as *I would be selling fun.* I knew I would have to work some nights and weekends, but with Lexi away at college, I felt we could deal with it. Like any sales person, I am money-motivated, but Ray was moving in, so I felt I could deal with the cut in pay. I went with my heart, and not my head. I would fly to Dallas on Tuesday, May 16 for training.

May 13, 2017 was my birthday, but more important, our engagement party. When our friends, Jamie and Rob, became engaged right after Ray and I started dating, we threw an engagement party for them. They had been waiting six years to "pay us back." When I called Jamie to tell her we were engaged, the first thing I said was she could now have a party. Finally, the night had arrived. Approximately 35 people attended, including all four of our kids. Lexi brought her best friend, Abby Davis, to the party. It was a magical evening, and, on the way home, I said to Ray how very lucky we were.

Sunday was Mother's Day, and Lexi had to work at her job at a local restaurant, so Ray took her and me to breakfast. I spent the afternoon with Marshall at a newly opened entertainment district.

I am a big planner, and because I knew I would be super busy once I returned home from Dallas, on Monday morning I mailed Lexi's graduation announcements with invites to her party for our local friends. I also called the bed and breakfast where we wanted to have our wedding in 2018 and contacted a photographer. We wanted a small wedding with only our kids present.

We never remembered what we did that Monday night.

Chapter 2

In Dallas Training for My Dream Job

*"The only goal you can't accomplish is
the one that you don't go after!"*
– Vilis Ozols

Early Tuesday I flew to Dallas for training for my new job and new career. I had posted on LinkedIn that after selling security for exactly 23 years and 11 months, I was starting my dream job selling fun! I left on an early flight so I could be in Dallas to have lunch with my lifelong friend Julie, who lives there. Before I left, I put dinner in the crockpot and left a note for Lexi. After writing her instructions for dinner, I wrote on the back, "Be super careful. Love You!" She was asleep when I left, but I still kissed her goodbye. The sight of her sleeping in her bed, with her hair in a braid, stayed with me for a long time.

During lunch with Julie, she said to me, "Your life is perfect," and it was. All four kids were in a great spot: Ellie was married and had two beautiful kids; Marshall was a CPA and loved his job; Ray's son Vern owned his home and enjoyed his job as an engineer; and Lexi was graduating from high school and going to Virginia Tech. Ray had recently moved in and we were about to start a new adventure. We had boxes left to unpack, but that would happen soon.

Julie had errands to run, and I went with her. We went into this cute gift shop where she told me they had wonderful graduation party supplies. I wanted to buy quite a few things, but I didn't have a lot of extra room in my suitcase. I bought only napkins with a graduation cap and a tassel that said, "It's been fun, but I'm glad it's done." They still sit unopened in my pantry.

My new employer's headquarters building was outstanding. It was like a company in Silicon Valley with pool tables, free snacks and drinks, and a spectacular view of Dallas. I loved the training and the company. It is an extraordinary organization and I felt, despite the cut in pay, I had made the right decision.

On May 17, Lexi called me during our lunch break and, as I was looking out over Dallas, she asked if she could go to a prom on Saturday. I told her yes, but I wouldn't buy her another dress. I had just spent a ton of money on a dress for her school's senior prom that was in a few weeks. I texted Ray and told him about it, and not to buy her another dress. He has a hard time saying no to her. I asked him to take photos for me because I wouldn't be there. I hated not being there for important moments like this, but I wasn't flying home until late Saturday night.

Thursday night, the 18th, Lexi told Ray she was skipping school and going to the beach the next day. When he asked her, "Do you think that is a good idea?" she said, "Yes."

Chapter 3

The Life-Changing Crash

"The devil whispers, 'You can't withstand the storm.'
The warrior replies, 'I am the storm.'"
– Unknown

The girls went to the beach, and when they ran into some other people from their high school, they hung out with them. One of the girls asked Lexi and Abby to leave to go to lunch, but Abby said no. They were going to enjoy the day until about three. They had to leave then because Abby had to get to her job, and Lexi wanted to attend a friend's birthday dinner.

It was sunny and beautiful outside—so weather wasn't a factor. According to Liz, a woman who witnessed the crash, the furniture delivery truck was weaving and driving erratically for at least two miles. Liz told her daughter, who was driving, to go around the truck as soon as she could as she was scared. Not long after they passed the truck, she saw the truck go off the right side of the road. It moved along a ditch line, then veered hard left. As it headed into oncoming traffic, one side lifted off the ground and slammed head on into Abby's SUV. The time was 3:19 p.m. The truck was a fully loaded furniture truck, with an approximate weight of more than 10,000 pounds. The truck turned on its side.

NOTE: I will never refer to the driver who killed Abby and so severely injured Lexi by name as to do so shows respect. I will not show him respect.

Here is how Liz (a nurse) described the crash:

When I ran to the crash scene, I was between both vehicles. The driver was climbing out of the wreckage. I spoke to him and saw his father (passenger) trying to disconnect his seatbelt, and I ascertained they did not need my help. At the same time, I realized I couldn't get to Abby and Lexi from where I was. So, I ran around the back of the truck (and the front of Abby's SUV) and pushed through the bushes to get to Lexi's side of the car.

As I was struggling to open the door, the truck driver came through the woods and stood beside me to my left. He said, "Oh shit, are they dead . . . are they dead?" and he moved away from the vehicle. Next, he started to move on the same side of the road as the accident towards my daughter's truck that was parked on the side of the road a few feet directly behind Abby's vehicle. After that, he started to run toward the farm across the street.

As I climbed into the back seat, I looked over the top of the car and saw a police officer giving chase and the driver running toward the fields behind the house. I never saw or heard of any civilians chasing him, only the police. When I was in the car, I checked Lexi's pulse and found it to be weak; however, her pupils were fixed and unmoving (which can happen in traumatic brain injuries) and she was breathing agonistically—labored and gasping—which is also sometimes called brain-stem breathing. I checked Abby's pulse more than once and could not find one; her pupils were also fixed and unmoving, and she was not breathing.

The whole time I was working, I was talking to them, telling them not to be afraid and that they weren't alone. When I realized Abby was dead, I said "Go in peace, sweet girl, don't be afraid," because most of us nurses believe when a person is dying their hearing is the last to go. I tried to move some of the glass from Lexi's face and chest. Then I quietly laid my hands on both of them for a moment because touch can be comforting.

This all happened in a flash . . . but those moments are burned in my brain, the heat and the smell of smoking vehicles, and oddly enough, the sun on the brown skin and blonde hair of two beautiful broken girls who were the same age as my child. All I kept thinking is what can I do for these girls: what would I want someone to do for my daughter? Medically, there wasn't anything I could do for them, but I tried to comfort them as best I could.

The dog in the backseat was wailing and making horrible noises. I reached as far as I could between the front seat and the back seat that were smashed together, but I couldn't reach the dog. As I heard the sirens of the approaching ambulance, I got out of the car and out of the way of rescue workers.

While all this was happening, my daughter had moved to stop the two girls who had been behind Abby's car because she knew it was something they didn't need to see. Both my daughter and I then stayed on the side of the road most of the afternoon with the girls trying to comfort them and reach you and Abby's parents.

Abby had been killed instantly. Lexi was hanging onto life by a thread, and the doctors didn't think she would make it through the night. I am sure they never saw the truck coming. If they had, Lexi would have instinctively covered her face, and her left arm wouldn't have been broken so badly.

The first officers to arrive at the scene found the driver hiding behind a nearby house. According to them, he smelled of alcohol, slurred his speech and had trouble standing. He failed three sobriety tests at the scene. He had marijuana, a prescription drug for anxiety, cocaine, and alcohol in his system at the time of the crash. His blood alcohol level two hours after the crash was between .10 and .11. The legal limit is .08. Abby's family later found cocaine at the crash site. The truck had bald tires and other maintenance issues. The driver had a long history of traffic violations and was driving on a suspended license.

Ironically, our school system participates in the Every Fifteen Minutes Program where one high school in the district acts out a horrific crash. The program was at the girls' high school exactly one week before the crash. Their friends who were behind them at the accident said it was like the Every Fifteen Minutes demonstration, but this was real— and one of their classmates and friends was dead.

The Every Fifteen Minutes Program is the last thing Lexi remembers before the crash. The Friday night after the program, I asked her how it was. She told me, "It was boring." I explained to her that graduation is a dangerous time of year, and every year a high schooler dies. She told me I was being dramatic.

Chapter 4

The Day That Changed Our Lives: May 19, 2017

"You never know how strong you are until being strong is the only choice you have."
— Cayla Mills

May 19 was a Friday, four weeks before graduation. Like all seniors (really all students), she was finished with her tests and nothing much was happening at school. She always saved up her absent days, which allowed her to go to the beach at the end of the school year. Our training started late that day in Dallas. I called Lexi, but she didn't answer. I called my mom in Salt Lake City and told her how happy I was with my decision. That day we were going to a venue in Dallas for training, and then to another location to eat dinner and play golf. I only took my wallet, so my purse with my keys, etc. were in my hotel room. Lexi texted me at 10:24 a.m. that she was going to the beach. I texted her back at 12:36 p.m. to put on lots of sunscreen. and asked if her friend's birthday dinner was happening that night. At 3:01 p.m., when I sent a text to ask if she was at the beach, she immediately responded, "Yes."

During training, my phone was plugged into the wall because my battery was dying and I had turned it on vibrate. I didn't see the call come in. We finished early, and I checked my phone and saw that Lexi's friend Brooke had called me. She never calls me. I listened to the message: "Lexi and Abby have been hit by an 18-wheeler." I tried to call her back, but there was no answer. I texted her at 3:50 p.m.: "Call me ASAP, Debbie." My new co-workers started trying to get me a flight home. At 3:55 p.m., I called Brooke again, and Liz, a nurse who had witnessed the crash, answered Brooke's phone. She said a blue SUV was involved in a crash and asked me if my daughter was the driver. I said no, it was Abby's car, and she would have been driving. She told me the passenger had a faint pulse, and the driver didn't. She must have told me that the passenger was being flown to the local Level-1 trauma hospital. I remember looking down at my hands that were shaking uncontrollably.

I called my fiancé and son, and neither one answered on my first try. When I finally reached Ray, he was walking out of work. When I reached my son, he was going to yoga. He instead drove to the hospital, which is about five minutes from his apartment. When he pulled into the parking lot, they were taking Lexi out of the helicopter. I know from the police report that was 4:20 p.m.

When we left for the Dallas airport, I remember waiting for the elevator and shaking all over. I was in a state of shock and thinking no matter what, my life had changed forever.

That Friday was beautiful and perfectly sunny when the crash happened. However, as often happens in Virginia, there were bad thunderstorms later that afternoon. Ray left work a few minutes after four, and usually it would have taken him an hour to get to the hospital, but it was 6:19 p.m. when he arrived due to the storm.

I kept calling my son who was at the ER. Both Abby and Lexi had long, blonde hair and looked similar, but Abby was much taller. I kept asking him to make sure it was Lexi at the hospital. He reassured me that he saw Lexi when she was taken off the helicopter. He told me they were doing a scan to make sure there was no internal bleeding. I had recently watched a movie about Princess Diana and how she looked fine after her car crash but died of internal bleeding. That is what I focused on. I remember telling him to make sure the hospital did everything they could to save her—*I needed her to live!*

At some point a friend gave me a number to reach Abby's dad, Steve Davis. I called him to tell him about the crash. I remember later Steve called me and told me he was at the crash scene, but they wouldn't let him get close. I told him the girls were airlifted to the hospital and to get there as soon as possible. He was hysterical because he couldn't get ahold of his wife, Terri. I called my friend Nichole and asked her to go to the hospital. I needed someone there on my behalf who was a mom.

It took us a while to get to the airport due to Dallas traffic on a Friday afternoon, and because we didn't know where we were going; none of us were from Dallas. I remember the driver, my co-worker, saying, "I'm sorry it's taking so long." I was on the phone at various times during the drive. My employer had booked me on a Southwest flight going through Baltimore. There were bad storms all over the East Coast. As they dropped me off at Love Field, a text said my flight was delayed until nine p.m. I went up to the Southwest ticket counter at Dallas Love Field and told the woman I needed to get home and to see if there were any other flights. They had nothing because so many flights had been cancelled. While I was standing at the ticket counter trying to figure out what to do, my friend Kristen called me. I asked her to find me another flight. When she called, I told her, "Lexi is alive," Kristen thought, "of course," not realizing how bad the crash was. She found one first-class ticket on a direct flight out of another airport, Dallas Fort Worth; it was the only seat left and cost $1600. It was scheduled to leave at 6:30 p.m. I had to get to the DFW. I cancelled the flight on Southwest and grabbed a cab. I remember Kristen calling to tell me I had to pay for the ticket once I reached the airport. Luckily, getting to DFW traffic wasn't too bad for a Friday afternoon, and I made it. When I told the cab driver what was going on, he wasn't going to charge me for the ride, but I said no and paid him. Once at DFW, the woman at the ticket counter gave me a hard time and said she couldn't find the reservation. I was panicking. At that point I was willing to pay any amount to get home or else I would have had to charter a plane. Finally, she found the reservation and took my credit card.

I was in such a state of shock. While walking to the gate, the manager from Lexi's restaurant job called me, and I told him Lexi wouldn't be at work because she was in an accident, then I hung up. I called my mom and my ex-husband from the airport. I kept calling my son to see if he had any news, and Ray to see if he had arrived at the hospital. I also texted or talked to a few of Lexi's friends. I texted my new boss at 5:59 p.m. and told her Lexi had no internal bleeding, she was on a breathing tube, and was being treated for possible brain damage.

One of Lexi's friends texted me and told me Abby was "NOT OK. Of course, I knew she was most likely dead.

Thank God I never looked at the news reports. I haven't yet seen how bad the crash was.

I had no idea how many people were at the hospital, but apparently there were hundreds of kids and their parents, as well as the high school principal. Ray told me when he arrived at the ER the crowd parted. He saw Lexi's good friend Emma; they hugged and cried. We had taken Emma with us to Lexi's 16th birthday trip to Universal Studios, so they knew each other well. Ray and Marshall were escorted into a private room. He thinks the police came in and talked to them. Shortly afterwards they went up to the sixth floor ICU. When I talked to Ray, he told me that he and Marshall were with Lexi in the burn trauma unit. I screamed, "Is she burned?" I hadn't even thought of that. I was in a full-fledged panic mode at that moment. He said no, and she looked okay, considering.

When I was talking to Nichole once she arrived at the hospital, she told me they had all heard a horrific scream from the room Steve Davis was in. The doctor had told him Abby was gone. I have heard from other people who were there that they were haunted by that scream for months. At the sentencing hearing, Terri, Abby's mother, talked about how long it took her to get to the hospital when she walked in, she knew Abby was gone by the look on everyone's face.

The chaplain from Virginia Beach police was at the ER as well, as the chaplain from the hospital. Many days later when I met with the hospital chaplain, she said the police were there as they didn't know what would happen, but she had never seen such an outpouring of love, and everyone was so well behaved. She felt that spoke volumes about how much the girls were loved.

May 19, 2017 was a deja vu moment. On January 10, 2003, I was at work and received a call on my cell. The caller ID said "Dad." My 95-year-old grandmother had fallen and broken her hip in early December, and they told my dad she would live only about six weeks. When I saw my dad was calling, I was expecting him to tell me that Grandma was gone. Instead it was my sister, asking,

"Have you talked to Dad's doctor?" I said no. Well, that morning he was in a single-car accident right outside the entrance to their condo. We think his SUV slid on black ice and slightly hit a tree. My dad didn't believe in seatbelts. I made him buckle up when he was with me, but he would always complain about how seatbelts weren't effective.

He should have walked away without a scratch from this accident, but because he didn't have a seatbelt on, his body flew, and he broke his neck. No one saw the accident, but someone had driven by and saw the SUV on the side of the road, and when he came back about 20 minutes later, he stopped and saw the body in the back of the SUV. He called 911. Dad's heart had stopped, but they revived him and took him to the ER. I left the office after this call, and my secretary was trying to get a flight for me and my kids back to Salt Lake City. Right after I left, the doctor called me and told me my dad had been without oxygen for an estimated 20 minutes so they were going to transfer him to a Level-1 trauma unit. They wanted to transport him by helicopter but were unable due to heavy fog; instead they moved him by ambulance. I remember the doctor didn't give me much hope. My dad was 72.

Once home, I packed clothes for us, and called Marshall's school asking that he wait at the office for me. When I picked him up from school, I told him about his Grampie's accident. Lexi was too little to understand. We headed to the airport. I remember I called my mom's best friend and left her a message about my dad's accident and asked if she could pick me up at the airport. When we were changing planes in Atlanta, my mom's friend called me back and said she and her husband would be there to pick us up. On the flight from Atlanta to Salt Lake City, the pilot announced they didn't know if they would be able to land. The fog was heavy in Salt Lake City, and a medical helicopter had crashed at the Salt Lake Airport and the crew had been killed, so it was shut down. I was in a panic mode. Although I knew my dad had been without oxygen for 20 minutes, I was afraid he would die before we could get there. The helicopter that crashed was the one they had wanted to put my dad on earlier that day. We finally landed in Salt Lake. When we arrived at the hospital about midnight, my dad was on life support in the ICU. I spent some time with him, but then my mom, sister, and I with my kids went home to try to sleep. I couldn't sleep. I knew he was gone. He had broken his neck and would have been paralyzed in addition to having severe brain damage due to lack of oxygen. I spent that time writing his obituary. My ex-husband's brother came and stayed with Marshall and Lexi the next morning, and my mom, sister, and I went back to the hospital.

The doctor pulled us into a small room and told us Dad was unresponsive, and there was no hope. Dad had repeatedly told us his biggest fear was living in a vegetative state after a stroke and he wouldn't want to live like that. Unfortunately, he didn't have a written "advance directive," which would have made it easier. We decided to pull the plug on what was keeping him alive. Because Mom didn't want to be in the room, she said her goodbyes, leaving my sister and me there when he stopped breathing. It was peaceful. I was always comfortable with our decision. Unfortunately, my dad's parents were both alive, and we had to tell them their only child was dead.

Now I was facing what could be a parallel outcome with my own 18-year-old daughter.

⌒⚘

Finally, I boarded the plane. I was in seat 1A and was first to board. I told the pilots my daughter had been in an awful accident, and I needed to get home so anything they could do would be appreciated. Of course, it didn't help. I called Ray before we left and made sure Lexi was still alive. I would be out of touch for over two hours and was terrified. Despite my plea to the pilots, we left late and didn't make up the time in flight; we were about 15 minutes late landing. Lexi always wanted to fly first class because of the extra benefits, but for some reason that night, they had only cold sandwiches for first class. I took a photo of my food to show her. I don't remember if there was alcohol; there must have been, but if I had anything it was a glass of wine. I knew I needed to hold myself together. I told Marshall on the phone before I left to tell Lexi I was flying first class. I was in such a state of shock and felt so helpless. I cried and prayed on that flight. I held onto the thought that she was in the best place possible, having been flown to the Level-1 trauma unit. I knew she was getting the best care possible; for some reason, I never thought she would die. Much later I found out they didn't expect her to make it through the night.

Before the plane took off, Ray had arranged for Nicole to pick me up. When we landed, I literally ran through the airport to her car, and she took me to the hospital. I don't remember the ride except she said all the girls' friends were staying the night at her house. When she dropped me off at the hospital, she hugged me and said, "Go get your daughter."

Chapter 5

The Sixth Floor: A Critical Time

"I'm realistic. I expect Miracles."
– Wayne Dyer

When I walked into the hospital, I had to show my ID because it was late. I texted Ray that I was there at 11:17 p.m., eight hours after the crash. The sixth floor was the burn trauma ICU and the neuro ICU. It is a place you never want to be. The hospital was under construction, and a countdown board sat next to the elevator. That is how I counted the days during our hospital stay. Looking back, it is mostly a blur, but Ray was at the elevator when I arrived, and we were buzzed into the ICU. Lexi looked like a tiny, broken doll. She had a tube down her throat, and her arm was wrapped up. Her face wasn't hurt but was almost completely covered by the tube in her nose and the plastic holding the tube down her throat. She had blood and cuts on the top of her forehead. She had a cut straight across her chest. It was beyond every parent's worst nightmare, but at least she was alive.

I talked to Lexi and told her I was back from Dallas and I had flown first class. Her friend, Emily, who I call my second daughter, had stayed at the hospital with her dad until I arrived. She was out in the waiting room. I remember hugging her and telling her to go home and get some sleep. At this time, it was probably midnight. The doctor knew I was flying in and had stayed late to see me. The doctor, Ray, and I went into a small room; Marshall stayed with Lexi. I had my training notebook with me, and I wrote down what the doctor told us, the first of many notes. She had severe injuries; no bleeding on her brain; no vascular injuries, but she had an air pocket on the left side of her lung; they were cooling her down; organs looked okay; many small pelvic fractures; her left arm was broken; she had a left pupil bloom and possible optic nerve damage; her heart rate was high; blood pressure low.

Earlier that night about 150 of the girls' friends had gathered at a local church. The local newspaper that covered the story said there was stunned silence as well as ragged sobbing. Lexi was in a group called Young Life, and one of the leaders their asked God to help them find hope. I found out about this afterwards. My heart was breaking, not only for Abby's family and us, but for all the girls' friends. Everyone's lives had changed forever.

Day 2: Saturday, May 20th

After the update, Ray and Marshall went home to sleep, and I stayed with Lexi. My outside world totally stopped, and my life became that small hospital room for the next several weeks. At one point about two a.m., a priest from the hospital came in and wanted to know if I wanted to pray with him. I remember telling him I wasn't that religious, but I had been praying more in the last few hours than I had in my entire life. I asked him to pray with me as he might have a more direct line to God. He smiled, and we prayed.

I am quite a talker, but I talked to Lexi like I never had before. I told her I was there and that I loved her. I talked about my first-class flight, the horrible cold food on the flight and all about Dallas. I talked about how wonderful she was, and how she was going to have the life both she and I had worked hard for her to have for 18 years. We are big Harry Potter fans, and I told her Harry Potter survived due to his mother's love, and she would survive because of my love.

At four a.m., 10 doctors were in her room, and they did a lung x-ray, heart scan, and a CAT scan. At five a.m., they had to drain her lung. At eight a.m., the neurosurgeon came in and said there was small bleeding in her brain, her left pupil was not reacting, and she had optic nerve or brain stem injury. The doctor explained she had a diffuse axonal injury (DAI). She needed to have an MRI but wasn't stable enough. I was told it would be a "very long road, and it was impossible to say for sure what the outcome would be." Her neurological exam "wasn't good." I wrote down, "significant TBI." At 8:30 a.m. a feeding tube was inserted. They were trying to stabilize her. I was barely able to breathe, let alone process what they were telling me. I have never been that scared. I would have given anything to be in that bed instead of her.

This is how BrainandSpinalCord.org describes diffuse axonal injury: diffuse axonal injury occurs in about half of all severe head traumas, making it one of the most common traumatic brain injuries. It can occur in moderate and mild brain injury. A diffuse axonal injury falls under the category of a diffuse brain injury. This means that instead of occurring in a specific area, like a focal brain injury, it occurs over a more widespread area.

In addition to being one of the most common types of brain injuries, it's also one of the most devastating.

Severe diffuse axonal injury is one of the leading causes of death in people with traumatic brain injury.

What Are the Causes of Diffuse Axonal Injury?

Diffuse axonal injury isn't the result of a blow to the head. Instead, it results from the brain moving back and forth in the skull because of acceleration or deceleration, which can happen in the following ways:

- Automobile accidents

- Sports-related accidents

- Violence

- Falls

- Child abuse such as Shaken Baby Syndrome

When acceleration or deceleration causes the brain to move within the skull, axons, the parts of the nerve cells that allow neurons to send messages between them, are disrupted. As tissue slides over tissue, a shearing injury occurs. This causes the lesions that are responsible for unconsciousness, as well as the vegetative state that occurs after a severe head injury.

A diffuse axonal injury also causes brain cells to die, which causes swelling in the brain. This increased pressure in the brain can cause decreased blood flow to the brain, as well as additional injury. The shearing can also release chemicals, which can contribute to additional brain injury.

I have two wonderful friends both named Jamie. One lives in California, and I will call her Aunt Jamie as that is what Lexi calls her. My other best friend Jamie lives locally. She and her husband held our engagement party for us a week before the crash.

Jamie texted me at 4:56 a.m. and said she and her

husband were available if we needed anything. I asked her to call her attorney and get a referral. Her daughter had worked in the emergency room where Lexi was. She had checked and told me Lexi had the "A team" in both the helicopter and the ER. I held onto that information like a lifeline for many months. At 6:51 a.m. she texted me they had seen the story on the local news and that no names were mentioned, but that one teen died and the other was fighting for her life. She said a ton of charges had been filed, and they believed there would be more.

I am a news junkie and like to watch the various local news reports. It was the lead story on the news for many, many days. It was extremely hard for me to watch. I always have looked away when they showed the crash because I didn't want to see the crushed car. For some reason, this story grabbed a great deal of attention. Maybe it was because they were both young and beautiful with such a promising future. It was also random as they were simply in the wrong place at the wrong time.

That first morning I texted Lexi's friends and told them not to come to the hospital and to pass the word on. I don't remember much about that first day; we were all in a state of shock. I received many text and Facebook messages that I didn't respond to as I was too overwhelmed.

At one point that day, Ray and I were outside in the waiting room and he said, "We need to get married." He explained if we were married, he could use his Family Medical Leave Act (FMLA), and Lexi could have additional insurance as well. At first, I didn't think he was serious, but he was. I kept asking him if he was sure he wanted to marry me; we didn't know what would happen with Lexi. I had been her primary caregiver her entire life—and that wouldn't change now. After asking him many times if he was sure, he told me to stop asking or he wouldn't marry me.

Jamie and her husband, Rob, came up and brought coffee and donuts that afternoon, and we were able to sit down for a few minutes. We took the coffee and donuts to the nurses, the first of many food items we had for them.

> **This was my post on Facebook:**
> *May 20, 2017 – Time: 5 a.m.*
> This is the best way to give updates. My beautiful daughter, Lexi, was involved in a horrific car crash yesterday. She is in the ICU, they are taking her for a CAT scan soon but here is what I know now. She has severe injuries. The main concern is traumatic brain injury. I was in Dallas when the crash occurred, thanks to my friends who helped me get home. I know how many people were at the hospital and I am grateful, however PLEASE do not come. No one can see her but family. I will post updates when I have them. Please send prayers for Lexi and her friend who did not survive the crash.

Later that day I posted again on Facebook with a photo of the two girls at my engagement party. My comment was, how I wish I could turn back time.

Marshall lives about five minutes from the hospital so I basically moved into his apartment. I slept there a few nights but also would go to try to nap as I wasn't sleeping much at night. One of the nurses, Ann, told us to get some sleep while Lexi was in ICU. She explained the ratio of patient to nurses in ICU is very good, thus they get lots of care. Once she goes to step-down care, someone would need to be there all the time. Thank God I listened to Ann; she was very right.

Because of the wars and the military, treating traumatic brain injuries has significantly advanced in the last 14 years.

They had Lexi on a cooling tube for the first week. The cooling tube helps to regulate your body temperature as your brain can not. After the first week they remove the tube and put the patient on cooling blankets. This is part of the standard protocol for traumatic brain injuries.

Marshall was going to stay the night in the hospital with her, so I went home. I hadn't slept since waking up Friday morning in Dallas. Driving home that Saturday night Ray said to me, "I am not one to ask for help, but this is way bigger than we can handle. We are going to need help." I agreed that no one could handle something like this without a lot of love and support.

That night there was a small gathering at the pond in our neighborhood that a few of Abby and Lexi's friends organized. Ray and I stopped by on our way home. Abby's parents were there, and we hugged and cried together. It was the first time I had seen them. They were devastated—it was hard to look at them. I also saw Kristen and her daughter Katie, who had been Lexi's childhood best friend, as well as a few of Lexi's other friends. I hugged them and cried and cried. It was all very hard. Everyone said how strong I was, but I was barely functioning. It was all I could do to put one foot in front of the other. I wanted nothing more than to curl up in a ball and sleep, and later to wake up and have this all be a bad dream.

Day 3: Sunday, May 21st

I spent that night at home but couldn't sleep. I was downstairs when the hospital called at 3:30 a.m., and I didn't have my phone with me. When I saw the hospital had called, I panicked. I called them right back, barely able to breathe. Luckily, Lexi only needed blood, and they had to get my okay.

I felt guilty, but I knew there was no way I could have

stopped her from going to the beach that day. Even if I had been home and told her no, she would have gone anyway. I would have had to lock her up to stop her. If only they had left the beach earlier to go to lunch with their friend or if only they had left five minutes later, it wouldn't have been them, but I cannot live my life thinking this way. It is not her fault or Abby's; *they were just at the wrong place at the wrong time.*

I packed some things to take to the hospital and to Marshall's house. I wanted to have things at the hospital that she could feel and smell to help stimulate her brain. I took essential oils to rub on her and for her to smell. I also took some spices for the smell, and I took a Harry Potter book. As I have mentioned, Lexi and I are huge Harry Potter fans. Lexi has read the books and seen the movies many times. I have always said they are magical books since my son was not a big reader until we read Harry Potter when he was 10. Ever since then, he has been a voracious reader. I have always told people Harry Potter books were magic for our family as they turned Marshall into a reader. I was hoping for more magic.

My Facebook post that morning:
May 21, 2017 – 7 a.m.
Last night Marshall took the night shift—I hadn't slept since Friday morning in Dallas. We stopped by the candlelight vigil for the girls last night for a few minutes. Lexi was supposed to be at East's prom last night. She had laid out possible jewelry and her dress. I also found her to-do list. My heart is broken. I will post an update when the doctors have been in.

My Facebook post later that morning:
May 21, 2017 – 8:20 a.m.

Lexi update. The doctors have done their
rounds. She needed some blood last night as
her hemoglobin was low. She is stable. She
made slight progress with the neurologist.
Keep praying and wish for any and all miracles.
Please know how much all of us appreciate the
posts and wishes and prayers. Please know I
read everything but can't respond to them all.
We are feeling the love.

Ray's kids, Vern and Ellie, and her husband David
and their two babies, were all out of town when the crash
happened. They offered to drive back the night of the crash,
but Ray told them no. They returned the next day and
brought us both lunch and dinner. This was the first of
many "family" dinners in the waiting room of the ICU on
the sixth floor. As Vern has said, "Couldn't we have had
a rousing game of monopoly as a family bonding time?"
What we were experiencing was beyond anyone's worst
nightmare; however, it did draw us all much closer.

I took notes every day. At one point someone at the
hospital told me: "You are going to need more paper."
That is when it dawned on me this wasn't going to be over
anytime soon. I remember one of my friends said maybe
Lexi might be in a wheelchair for graduation in four weeks.
Oh, how I wish that had been the case.

Lexi had sand from the beach in between her toes.
Although she loves the beach, she hates being sandy. As
tears rolled down my face, I brushed the sand off her toes,
talking to her the entire time.

Here are my notes from that day:
Orthopedic surgeon was in, and Lexi's left
elbow is fractured and will need surgery. They
want her neurological condition to improve

before they operate. She will probably have limited range of motion and maybe arthritis, *but we can live with that.* No timeline for surgery right now, but doctors will keep us posted. She opened her eye yesterday when they pulled tape off. They would do an MRI when stable.

I learned from witnesses that Abby's puppy, Macy, was in the back seat behind Abby. Lexi was reaching back petting the puppy when the crash happened. That is how her arm became so badly broken. I know they never saw the truck coming at them, and they never knew what hit them, that gives me some peace. Abby died instantly. The dog didn't survive the accident either.

Numerous doctors from all over the country have looked at her arm X-rays and said they have never seen such damage. The surgeon who finally performed the surgery had been a trauma doctor for 30 years, and this was the only time he had ever fused an elbow.

I remember being in her hospital room alone with Marshall, and we were both afraid she would never wake up. We hugged, and I was crying; I am not sure if he was as well. He said, "She wouldn't want to live in a vegetative state." That was a very real possibility.

May 21st was Ray's birthday. He told Lexi that morning it was his birthday, and he told her all he wanted for his birthday was for her to give him a thumb's up or squeeze his hand. Right then she squeezed his hand. He said it is the best birthday present he has ever had.

That Sunday afternoon I called the Davises and spoke to Steve and Terri. I remember saying to them that we were both on different but very difficult paths. I remember I told them about the doctors saying she might have arthritic pain in her arm for the rest of her life, and how I could live with that. We all laughed. They talked about not being able to get Abby's body until Monday, and how upset they were. I believe it was that phone call where we talked about what to bury Abby in. Her favorite dress was a short-sleeve blue dress, but the coroner said she needed to have something with sleeves. I suggested her graduation gown.

I couldn't begin to wrap my head around the fact that Abby was gone.

That Sunday, Ray told me I needed to call my best friend in California, Aunt Jamie. I said I didn't want to because that would make it real. One time when Lexi was little, she asked how we were related. I said we weren't, but if I could choose a sister it would be Jamie. Although Lexi had set Jamie up on Facebook years ago, she never used it, meaning she had no way to know about the crash. Jamie and I didn't talk long that afternoon, but she said she was there if we needed her.

I did a phone interview with the press. When the reporter asked if I could send photos of Lexi, I said, "Yes, how many? I have a million." That night the girls' friends had organized a balloon release at the high school football stadium. At the last minute I decided to go. They had tables set up to write notes on the balloons and write notes to Lexi and the Davises. The outpouring was overwhelming. I estimate a thousand people were there. I met Abby's grandparents, the first of many sad occasions.

Day 4: Monday, May 22

My posting on Facebook:
As I wake up on the first Monday of a "new normal," I am most grateful for the love and support. Saturday night driving home, Ray said he is used to dealing with problems alone, and I have done that too. We know this is the

biggest problem we and our families have ever faced, and I promise you we will be reaching out to everyone who has offered to help at some point in this long road. Hug your loved ones tight. I cherished the hugs Lexi gave me last weekend for my birthday and Mother's Day, but they mean even more now.

My notes:
She is on 21 percent oxygen, has a tube in her left chest to drain the fluid, and her pupils haven't changed. Her temperature is good. She has been heavily sedated, and they are going to try to back that off to see if she would respond. The main doctor said, "All things considered, she is good."

That morning I looked up and saw outside the hospital room door a friend of mine who is a pediatrician. I hadn't seen Natalie in years, but we had both been on the board of a literacy charity. We were Facebook friends, and I am guessing she had seen my post. My last name was different than Lexi's, causing many people to not make the connection. It was sweet of her to stop by. We chatted briefly. She became a medical resource I used on our journey.

In a weird coincidence, our hairdresser Annette's husband was a patient at the same time in the ICU across the hall. He was there fighting a brain tumor. She had heard about Lexi and sent me a text that she was there. We met in the hall between our respective units for a big hug. As every woman knows, our hairdresser is an important part of our lives. After six years, we considered her a good friend.

Kristen texted to ask if she could start a crowd-funding page to help with the medical costs. I was beyond terrified about money. Although I had insurance, I had recently changed jobs, which was bad timing. I joked I met my high deductible with her $12,000 helicopter ride to the hospital. I had worried about how I had taken a significant pay cut to have my dream job. Now I wasn't sure if I would be able to even work, and we didn't know if we would need to move or have significant changes done to the house if Lexi could come home. Everything was extremely overwhelming, and money was a *huge* piece of that. I called the YMCA on Monday to cancel our membership; I cancelled our cable, the pest control service, and the newspaper delivery. I wanted to eliminate any unnecessary expense. I didn't know what the future would hold.

I am normally the organizer when someone is having a tough time, so I know how people want to help. A few years ago, a friend of mine had breast cancer and when I organized meals, she was reluctant to accept the help. I explained to her that people want to help and there will be a time when she can return the favor. Now I was the one needing help, and lots of it. I was and will continue to be incredibly grateful for all the love and support we received. Having the crowd-funding page with all the donations made our lives and getting Lexi every help that was available much easier. Although I would give every dollar back a million times over if it would get Lexi back to the way she was when she woke up on May 19th, the money made decision-making much easier.

I glanced at newly delivered flowers when I went home and discovered my new employer had sent them. My new boss was great: she didn't pressure me about returning to work. That was the last thing on my mind with everything else going on.

I had called the local Episcopal church and asked a priest to come to the hospital. He came over and we all prayed over Lexi's bed. After he was done, we were standing in the hospital room talking and he asked if he could do anything else for us. I said, "Can you do a quick wedding?" He said yes, and asked us where we wanted it: the hospital room, the hospital chapel, etc. The church was a block from the hospital, and I wanted a church wedding. We set the day and time around Lexi's surgery, tentatively scheduling it for the following Saturday.

Monday, I hired an attorney. I had checked with my friends over the weekend but ended up hiring an attorney who was interviewed on a local TV station after the girls' crash. I had seen him interviewed before. His name is Mike, and while he was in law school his brother was killed by a drunk driver. He is involved in the local Mothers Against Drunk Drivers (MADD) chapter and has done a lot of work with drunk-driving cases. I felt drunk-driving cases were a passion for him and that is what I wanted. He gave me the number of a woman at MADD, so I could talk to her when I was ready. At that time, I had control over very little, but I was happy with my decision. He recommended I stop posting on Facebook for legal reasons. That was hard because it was how I was communicating with everyone. But I understood the furniture company's lawyers could and would use anything against us in court. I felt bad that a lot of people were freaking out when I said I couldn't post anymore.

Day 5: Tuesday, May 23

My notes:
I slept at home and was told Lexi had a good night. She did a peace sign and thumbs up and shook her head yes and no. She also opened one eye. I had to wait outside while they changed her diaper. So hard!

They may do an MRI today. Her chest

tube will stay in for surgery. She is following commands on her right side. She opened her right eye, but her pupils were unchanged. When I arrived this morning, she was thrashing around and grabbed my hand several times. She is obviously very agitated.

That morning I received a text from an executive at my new employer whom I had met when I was in Dallas, remember, I had only been with them for three days before the crash. Part of his text read, "Needless to say my thoughts and prayers are with you and your daughter. When I heard the news, my heart sunk. Bad things shouldn't happen to such good people. I can't imagine what you are going through, but I want you to know that we mean it when we talk about the corporate family. Whatever you need you let me know."

I didn't know what would happen with my job; it was hard to even think about. I thanked him, and said, "Her friend's family is planning a funeral, so it could be worse." I didn't walk into my new job for six weeks, but they held it for me, which says a lot about the company. I will always be forever grateful to everyone there.

One of the girls' friends sent me a text that all her friends were dressing up cute and going to the coffee shop before school like Lexi and Abby did every morning. That made me cry. I felt so bad for their friends. How do you handle something like this? I couldn't handle it. This should have been one of the most exciting times in their young lives, and they shouldn't have to deal with tragedy. All of this is because of some idiot who chose to drink and drive.

I saw on Facebook where the other schools were wearing the girls' high school colors to honor Abby and Lexi. Also, a mother told me her daughter's third grade soccer team was wearing ribbons for the girls. Even though life went on for others, everyone who knew the girls, and even total strangers, had been touched by the tragedy.

Because I couldn't post on Facebook per my attorney, I decided to send out a mass email to selected people. I was instructed to make certain nothing showed up on social media—so I made sure that everyone knew that on every email I sent. It was the best way I could think of to share some information.

The police chaplain came by and I was talking to him quietly. Every time we mentioned the crash, Lexi's blood pressure and heart rate changed, which told me she could hear us now. She also shook her head yes and no to simple questions.

They told us they might do surgery on her arm the next day, which could take eight to nine hours. Oh my God! They did the MRI and it came back "as expected showing sheering injury to her brain." I didn't ask for more details. The neurologist seemed pleased with Lexi's progress. They would probably put in a tracheotomy when they did the surgery. She was not conscious enough to make sure she could keep her airway open. She continued to thrash about sometimes and had opened her eye twice. I hoped that was a good sign.

That day, a story about the accident was the top headline on the front page. The local paper had wanted to interview someone and had contacted Kristen because she was the organizer of the fundraising page. I said her daughter Katie could talk to the paper. She did a great job, talking about how strong Lexi was and how if anyone could survive this, she could. The story traveled far and wide. When we were in Atlanta, other families came up to us and said they knew of our story.

I spoke to the principal of Lexi's high school. The first question I asked was, "Will she graduate?" I knew all tests were done, but I wanted to make sure she would graduate from high school. The principal was extraordinary, and a great support to our family. I can't imagine how hard it was to navigate the staff and students through this difficult time.

In the middle of all this, I was organizing a small wedding for us. I suggested what everyone would wear and ordered flowers for Ellie to pick up. Ellie asked if I needed anything else, like something old. I said everything else can wait for the real wedding. Ray responded I had him for *something old.*

On my notes for the 23rd, I had written down the name of the prosecutor and her phone number. I wrote: "She wants to discuss what to expect." I was about to go down the rabbit hole of the legal system.

I had received lots of emails, texts, and Facebook messages from family, friends, and people who knew Lexi. Unfortunately, I didn't see some of them for over a year as I was completely overwhelmed.

Below is a great example of a supportive email from my former sister-in-law who lives in Oregon:

> Debbie, thank you for including me in this list. It is hard to watch something like this from a distance and know that only my words can help support you. But I hope you can feel my *huge hugs* in those words. What a sad statement on society that you are forced *to cover your ass* for something so tragically and obviously someone else's fault, but I agree it's a good idea to take it off line. Her moving and responding (a peace sign—love it!) are all positive and I'm sure heartening to see. But it will be a long-time healing with lifelong impact not only on her, but all those around her. It is very nice to see such strong community and school support.

It's obvious she is loved.

Having gone through something like this with my step-son, my advice is to accept the help people offer. Being kind of a private person, I found it hard to let go, but your one friend who said for friends to go do whatever they see needs to be done, and not burden you with having to think, was perfect. It's important that your focus remain on Lexi.

I'm not a praying person, but you know my healing energy is focused on her and I'm sending strength to you, Marshall, and Ray. I know the days ahead will be long and difficult. Know that my heart is with you. Wish I could do more. Love you.

Day 6: Wednesday, May 24

Notes from doctor's rounds:
She opened her eyes spontaneously last night. Her left pupil was sluggish. They are going to do a lung ultrasound. They put a tube down her throat at the crash scene that enabled her to breathe, and she has been on a respirator to help her breathe. They want to get the tube out because the longer it is in, the greater the risk of infection and throat damage. They will put in the trach tomorrow. Her arm surgery is scheduled for Friday if they can get her on the schedule. It is critical but not an emergency.

This was the day that the case manager came in and had me fill out forms to get Lexi on Social Security Disability and Medicaid. She was 18 and liked to tell me a million times a day, "I'm an adult." The good thing about that is she would be responsible for her bills. I knew the medical flight she took to the hospital had met my deductible, and I was freaking out about the cost.

I returned as many items as I could. We had dropped her prom dress off at the alterations shop right before I went to Dallas. I called and they hadn't done anything to the dress yet, so I had her friend pick it up and return it to the dress shop. Friends also returned all the stuff for her graduation party.

Ray had given me tickets for Christmas to see Neil Diamond in Baltimore, so we had hotel reservations. We were planning on going up on Friday, seeing the concert and staying the night, then coming back for her graduation party. I cancelled the hotel reservations and unsuccessfully tried to sell the tickets online. I also had to cancel all the hotel reservations I had made to take her to college.

My world became the sixth floor of the hospital. Her room was quite small with the bed and one uncomfortable chair I sat in or tried to sleep in. I would pull the chair up to the bed and read to her. I stored all my spices and oils on the windowsill along with the Harry Potter book because there was no other place to put them.

Ray and I tried to keep track of the names of all the nurses who helped her, but there were too many of them— and we were overwhelmed. The nurses were absolutely wonderful. They took such great care of her and us as well. They would even bring me tea from their break room.

The waiting room on the sixth floor was where we had our family dinners and where we would go out to meet friends or take a phone call or a quick break. Until Lexi was out of ICU, only immediate family was allowed in her room. It was such a small space we couldn't have had many people in there anyway. One time when Ellie and David were there, I took our grandkids outside. I needed some air, and we didn't want our grandkids to see Lexi lying in the hospital bed unresponsive. The hospital is right next door to a children's hospital. When Lexi had pneumonia in February of 2016, we took her to the emergency room at the children's hospital at the direction of her doctor. Two days later we found out she also had mononucleosis. It lasted for months. I looked back on when she had pneumonia and mononucleosis as a fond memory, compared to what we were going through now.

Day 7: Thursday, May 25th

This was one of the scariest days. When we arrived at the hospital, she was neurostorming.

Neurostorming is when patients with a low level of neurological activity start going into chaos. Their blood pressure goes crazy, their temperature can fluctuate, and they can move in strange ways. It was terrifying.

I am a great believer that knowledge is power, however because I could barely put one foot in front of the other, I hadn't done any research. Apparently, my son had, because he knew what neurostorming was. He told me it could go on for a long time. I was beyond terrified. This is what I feared more than anything—her having no control over her body, and never coming out of the coma. I have never been more fearful in my life.

During rounds that morning I took the following notes:
Her stats were not great; they are at the lower end of normal. Yesterday she was mostly breathing on her own; today she needs help. She was not following commands this morning. Left pupil is bad. The lower left lobe of her

chest has a cloud; they will do an x-ray. Her lower left leg had a lump; another x-ray needed. The main doctor told me "I would like her more awake, more consistently awake."

They tried to do a tracheotomy that morning, but her lung pressure dropped too low. Since she was sedated, Ray and I ran out to get wedding rings. When we walked into the local jewelry store, I said, "We need wedding bands quickly." Ray said, "She's pregnant!" We all laughed because I was a little too old to be pregnant. We found a ring that so perfectly matched my engagement ring you would think they were made for each other. I said that was our first miracle. Later, I found out that was the second one. The first miracle was that Lexi survived that first night.

At three p.m., the eye doctors came in. They carried their equipment in backpacks, making it easy to spot them. They said they may need to sew Lexi's left eye shut, but they would tape it for now. They told us there was damage to her brain stem and damage to her optic nerve. They said her vision might be poor in the left eye, but thought her right eye was okay. However, there was no way to know until she woke up.

In retrospect, I wish they had been right that she had lost vision in one eye.

That afternoon Kristen texted me saying that it looked like someone had done an update on Lexi's Facebook page. Obviously, she wasn't doing it, and whoever was didn't realize the connections I had to put a stop to postings. Aunt Jamie's son, Chris, had worked for Facebook, and I knew he could help. I texted his mom, but when she didn't respond after five minutes, I had Marshall contact him. Marshall and Chris had been friends their entire lives, and they were friends on Facebook. Marshall was able to Facebook message him and obtained the information we needed. Unfortunately, because she was 18, we couldn't make any changes without getting guardianship. Another thing to add to my list. Fortunately, I found her passwords a few days later and was able to change the password right away, because it would take a month or more to get guardianship.

Day 8: Friday, May 26th

Notes from doctor's rounds:
Her neurostorming has died down, and she had a good night. Hallelujah! Because her eye also looks better, they are going to continue with the tape. She is off the cooling machine and her surgery is scheduled for 7:30 p.m. tomorrow. She is responding to pain. Her movement before was a 6 and now it's only a 5. They think her cooling tube was infected. At two p.m. her fever is 103 degrees.

This was the day of Abby's funeral. I had asked Kristen earlier in the week if she could come sit with Lexi while I attended the funeral. That morning, I realized there was no way I could sit through it. I couldn't absorb the fact that Abby was gone. I was in pure survival mode. I texted a friend and asked her to tell the Davises I was sorry that I couldn't be there. It was hard to believe how our lives had changed in a week. Her funeral was the lead story on the news. Hundreds of people were there, including some of the first responders. The middle school where both girls went was between the church and the cemetery, and all the students came out and lined the street as the funeral procession went by. Again, the love from our community was above and beyond anything I could imagine. It would be months before I could wrap my head around the fact that Abby was gone. I couldn't get up the courage to go to her grave for six months.

A few days earlier, I had texted Ray's sister, Olga, about how Lexi was doing. She had been in Virginia the previous Thanksgiving and had bonded with Lexi. She had taken her shopping and they had so much fun. She has two boys and loved spending time with Lexi, who is a total girl. I mentioned that we were getting married on Saturday. When Ray found out I had mentioned the wedding, both he and Vern said, "She will be here for the wedding." I said, "No way," as it was just a few days away. Well, my soon-to-be sister-in-law was flying in from California. I hadn't been home for a week and Lexi's bathroom was always a mess. I joked that I clean the bathrooms once a week, whether they need them or not. With all the makeup she wears, Lexi's sink was a mess and there was more shampoo on the walls of her tub than in her hair. Obviously, I couldn't leave to clean, and when I texted my friend Rhonda, she and her daughter came over and cleaned. They did a great job but, unfortunately, they straightened up Lexi's room. The few times I had been home were awful. I missed her very much and badly wanted her back in her own bed the way I had left her on Tuesday, May 16th. When I saw they had made Lexi's bed and picked up her room, I became hysterical. I should have told them to leave it, but it didn't even cross my mind. I didn't want to move anything—so that when she came home, it would be the same.

Little did I know then how long it would be before Lexi came home.

The hospital's rehabilitation people came in to see Marshall and me. When they left, the nurse closed the door and told us that *we didn't want Lexi to be upstairs for rehab*. It was fine for 60-year-olds who suffered a stroke, but she needed to get to a specialized place. She said, "Get her to Shepherd Center in Atlanta. Miracles happen there." I walked out and called Shepherd Center. They had a wait list, but it looked like the week of June 5th they would have five beds open. Lexi needed to be stable enough to travel before we could do anything. I was praying everything would fall into place.

I was now in the world of rehab hospitals. It turns out the rehab hospitals must accept you. Of course, you must have insurance, but they also want to make sure you will get better. We had been told she would make the most progress the first six months—I felt that was the golden time, and I didn't want to waste one second. If she couldn't get into Shepherd Center, I wanted a backup plan. I did some research and called on some doctor friends and found out about Spaulding in Boston and TIRR Memorial Hermann in Houston, the hospital that Congresswoman Gabby Gifford went to after she was shot. I called all three admittance offices and had the social worker send the medical records to all three places. This process was over-whelming, but it gave me something positive to focus on. I have spoken to other families whose insurance wouldn't cover a specialized hospital. They were able to fight to get it covered, *so don't take no for an answer*!

We were turned down by Spaulding and we were on the list for TIRR Memorial Herman Hospital in Houston, Texas. Our first choice was still Shepherd Center. Atlanta was a lot closer than Houston. Once I knew for sure Lexi was accepted at the Shepherd Center, I cancelled the process at TIRR Memorial Hermann.

At one point the social worker came in and told me that some insurance companies won't cover the medical flight and it can be very expensive. I had noted that over $10,000 had been raised in 24 hours from the fundraising page. I was able to tell the social worker to book the flight, and we would deal with it if the insurance company wouldn't pay.

I had to give my credit card number just in case.

At 2:51 p.m., I texted our other children that Lexi had a blood infection, thus, no surgery for the next day. The "blood infection" was sepsis, a major killer. We were blessed that she was young and healthy—and had such a will to live. I told the others we would try to keep the wedding for Saturday at two p.m.

Day 9: May 27 – Our Wedding Day

In addition to everything else, I had managed to plan a small wedding. I ordered flowers, asked a friend to bring champagne, and organized what the men would wear. My friend Nichole was coming to stay with Lexi, and her daughter Waverly was going to be our photographer. Waverly had taken the photos that were now rather famous as they were Lexi's senior photos. Most of those photos were all over the news.

When I had talked to Ray from Dallas, I told him to tell the hospital he was her step-dad. We stuck with that story until we found out the nurse overheard us, so our cover was blown. At that point, because everyone at the hospital could tell how much Ray loved Lexi, nothing was ever said even though it was supposed to be only immediate family in her room. I tried to keep it quiet about the wedding, *but nurses know everything.*

Many of our friends had reached out to us and brought us food and other things. We were originally going to have only our kids at the wedding, but we ended up inviting a small handful of friends. In retrospect, I wish I would have reached out to a few more people, but it was incredible that I was able to accomplish what I did. I wore the white dress I had worn for our engagement party. I told the guys to wear blue shirts and black pants so they didn't need to buy anything.

We had to keep changing the time of the wedding because we thought Lexi would have surgery, but the surgery kept getting pushed back. At 7:30 the morning of the wedding, I finally confirmed the time with the reverend. That morning when I told Lexi that Ray and I were getting married, she opened her good eye. Nichole came to stay in the ICU with her as Ray and I ran over to Marshall's apartment to get changed. Ray had grabbed his suit, but when we were changing, we realized he didn't have his pants. I called Lexi's friend Emily, who was coming to the wedding; because she hadn't left her house yet, she was able to run by and get the pants. I remember during our vows when I said for better or worse, I thought, *I hope it never gets worse than this.*

During the ceremony when the reverend said a prayer for Lexi, I choked back tears. This was not the wedding we had planned. She should have been by my side.

We had a small, quick reception in the church hall with a mix of three different kinds of champagnes that guests had brought. Ellie had made two incredibly beautiful cakes. It was a magical wedding, especially under the circumstances. My maid of honor, Jamie, said it was one of the most beautiful weddings she had ever seen. She felt there was so much love in the church. After the wedding, we ran back to the ICU and when I walked in the staff clapped. It was difficult not having Lexi there, but I was incredibly happy. I wrote in my journal that night, "If only Lexi would wake up now. The morning of your wedding you shouldn't be crying in the shower. I want my baby back!"

Unfortunately, she was not doing well.

My notes:
She has a torn cornea and low potassium. She hasn't responded to commands for two days. She needs more ventilator support than before.

She also has a strep infection or possibly septic infection and pneumonia. They are doing blood tests. They wanted her to be able to breathe on her own and follow commands before they would put in the trach. Apparently when someone has a breathing tube put in, especially out in the field by the first responders, they want to get it out as soon as possible as there is a high risk of infection.

Day 10: Sunday, May 28th

This day at home I found the note I had left for Lexi before I went to Dallas. The one where the front had directions about the dinner I had made for her and Ray. I don't think she ever turned the note over to see where I had written on the back, "Be super careful! Love You!" When I saw the note, I was beside myself. I have always been an insane worrier. For me the hardest part of being a parent was when my kids started driving. I am sure part of that is linked to my Dad having died in a car accident. I remember when Marshall could drive, I wouldn't let him drive with Lexi for at least the first year. When he would take her somewhere, I would tell him, "My entire life is in your car, be careful."

Notes from doctor's rounds:
She moved her head and looked at the nurse. She is breathing mostly on her own as the respirator is on the lowest setting. They are treating her with a broad-spectrum antibiotic; her temperature is 100.4. They told me again this is a long, slow road.

Day 11: Monday, May 29 – Memorial Day

She had her eye open when I arrived and *squeezed my hand*. I showed her my wedding ring. The physical therapists came in and showed me how to move her legs and feet—*at last I could do something*.

> **Notes from doctor's rounds:**
> Her eyes are the same, but she has a septic infection as well as pneumonia and high blood pressure. She is on day-four of antibiotics. They will keep her on antibiotics for 10 days. Mid-to-late week she would have surgery for her arm and may have the trach put in tomorrow. The doctor told me "She is making strides in the right direction," and "Once we started treating the infection, she is remarkably better."

The wonderful nurses gave her a bath. They have a stash of good-smelling body wash and shampoo they buy with their own money. They had to use a bedpan for her hair. They picked tons of glass out of her hair. I was scared because they were kind of rough on her head as they tried to clean it and brush it out. I didn't want them to cause any more brain damage. It took everything I had not to jump in and stop them—or to run screaming from the room.

The bath was very stimulating, so I wanted to let her rest. We left the hospital after the bath to get lunch and it really felt great to get back out into the world. I remember being shocked that everyone else's life was continuing. Ray and I and my new sister-in-law Olga went to a neighborhood right up the street from the hospital. After lunch we went into two shops, and I bought a sign saying, "Expect Miracles," an ornament saying, "Brave Girl," and a bracelet for healing. The bracelet package said to keep the bracelet on, and when it fell off, the person would be healed. It fell off before Lexi came home, *but it witnessed a lot of miracles.* I had the "Expect Miracles" sign and "Brave Girl" ornament in her hospital rooms. The "Expect Miracles" sign now stands next to her graduation photo in my family room.

We were learning about the community support from many different people. Brooke's dad and a bunch of other dads put Lexi and Abby's initials on the softball field before the game, and everyone loved it. My friend Nancy's dad passed away and she asked for donations to Lexi instead of flowers for her dad. A local pizza place had a fundraiser for both girls and they ran out of food by 7p.m.! The love and support we received from the community was a light in the darkest of days.

Day 12: Tuesday, May 30

Notes from doctor's rounds:
Severe TBI, she followed one or two commands last night, she opened her eyes spontaneously. Tracheotomy is scheduled for tomorrow. Her blood pressure and heart rate are better. Fever is neurologic due to the brain injury not the infection. Her cultures have been coming back ok. Day 5 of antibiotics. Surgery for her arm will be mid-to-late this week if her fever improves. If she wakes up enough after her arm surgery, she may not need the tracheotomy. Her veins are blown on her good arm, making it very hard to draw blood. They will try to get a vein in her foot. They will do a chest x-ray to make sure she doesn't have pneumonia.

She had a tattoo done on her thigh when she turned 18,

which she showed me after it was healed. The tattoo says, "This too shall pass." At four p.m. she opened both eyes—when the nurses and I were talking about how prophetic the tattoo was.

Day 13: Wednesday, May 31

I usually arrived at the hospital by six a.m. for rounds, and this is what I wrote:

> She is out of it this morning; they gave her "oxy" something at five a.m.

I was so afraid she would be in a vegetative state. Before the crash, when I would tell her to be careful or brought up the possibility of her ending up that way, she would say I was being "dramatic." This was a huge fear for me, like it had been for my dad. My vibrant, smart, beautiful daughter had lain mostly unresponsive for the 13th day. *I had never been this afraid in my life.* I was able to move her legs and give her things to smell, which made me feel better. The staff was so wonderful at the hospital and I knew she was getting the best care possible. She was already on the list at two rehabilitation hospitals, so when she would be able to travel, we could get her to the best rehab hospital. That was what I was focusing on.

At 4:40 p.m. they took Lexi to surgery for the tracheotomy. Ray and I walked down to the operating room with her. They wanted to put a trach in because the risk of infection goes up every day the tube is down her throat. If she needed help breathing, they could hook the trach up to the respirator.

The surgery went well, thank the Lord. She was asleep when she came back up to her room because of the medication. Because Olga was returning to California in the morning, she kissed Lexi goodbye when we left. We all went home to try to get some sleep.

Chapter 6

She's Awake: Day 14

*"No matter how dark the moment,
love and hope are always possible."*
– George Chakiris

Day 14: Thursday, June 1

Notes from doctor's rounds:
They told me she opened her eye spontaneously last night, and she is moving her upper left arm but not her lower arm. Chest x-ray shows mild pneumonia and she has a temp of 101.4. Urine sample shows a few white blood cells, but they are awaiting a full test. Planning on surgery on her arm tomorrow. They will lower her pain meds because they are affecting her heart rate. Day 6 of 10 on antibiotics. At 12:30 p.m. she has a fever of 101.1

BEST DAY YET! When I arrived at the hospital, Lexi's eye was open and she was grabbing with her good arm. The trach *made a difference.*

Lexi seemed to be coming out of the coma and they wanted us to be on a schedule with limited stimulation time and lots of downtime. It was important she didn't get too stimulated. We tried to stick to that schedule.

They continued having issues getting any good veins

in her right arm. Due to the damage, her left arm was not an option. They ended up putting an IV in her foot due to her collapsed veins in her arm. Her right eye was open. It looked like she was trying to move her lips. Her left eye was moving around and she was moving her left arm a lot. It seemed like she was trying to communicate.

The nurses picked her up and lifted her into a chair at 12:30 p.m., allowing her to sit up with some assistance. Her one eye was open. I was talking to her all the time and I knew she was listening. I kept waiting for her to ask me why I was out of the house looking as horrible as I did. She was my harshest critic when it came to what I was wearing. I looked and felt like I hadn't slept in a month. Every day I was throwing on any comfortable clothes I could find. She would have been mortified to see me in public the way I looked.

Because Lexi was in a Level-1 trauma unit, they got all the gunshot victims and other serious emergencies, which took precedence in the operating room. As a result, her surgery was constantly pushed back, and I was beyond furious. Our good friend Kathy worked for the hospital so I texted her and explained about Lexi's surgery getting bumped. I asked her: "Who do I need to raise hell with?" She emailed the president of the hospital about the surgery. In the same email, she mentioned the dirty bathrooms. For some reason we weren't allowed to use the bathroom in Lexi's room (she wasn't using it), and we had to go out to the hall or to the waiting room on to the first floor. All the bathrooms were filthy. This was a hospital, for God's sake. When I would leave Lexi's room, my biggest decision every day was which dirty bathroom to use. After Kathy told the hospital president about the dirty bathrooms, they did improve a bit.

I was driving Lexi's car on the way to Marshall's to take a quick nap, while pulling into the parking garage, I noticed Lexi's graduation tassel hanging from the rear-view mirror. The tassel caused me such pain I had to put it in her glove box where it stayed until I had to sell her car over a year later.

Late doctor's rounds:
No complications due to trach, swelling is coming down, and they will continue to monitor her blood pressure and heart rate. She is peeing! They will start tube feeding since they can't get her into surgery. Day 7 of 10 on antibiotics, last two cultures have been negative. The doctors said, "Doing very well on stats," and "Really happy with chest." She is medically able to travel. Off critical life support ventilation. Every step forward was a step in the right direction. We were happy for every baby step.

Looking back, once she had the trach, she started to respond. That was when she turned the corner and our prayers started to be answered.

Day 15: Friday, June 2

Notes:
Her neuro stats are improving a lot. There was a small amount of secretions from her lungs last night. No blood gas done, coarse breath sound on left side. Temp 99.5 had pain med a bit ago. Has a rectal laceration. They want to give her a good once-over, make sure they aren't missing anything. They are keeping the ventilator on overnight and then backing off during the day. "Heading in right direction."

Two weeks before, my world had crashed in around me. I thought I was sort of coming to terms with the enormity of this—although the hospital had been telling us from the beginning this will be a long road and to expect small improvements.

I received an email from Abby's mom. Although I was in a total state of shock, I couldn't imagine what they were going through. They wanted to come and see Lexi. In retrospect, I wish I would have let them come but I was afraid if she saw them, especially Terri, that it would trigger her memories of Abby because Terri and Abby looked so much alike. The Davises told me it would bring them comfort, so I tried to work it out that they could see her when she was asleep . . . but she *wasn't sleeping.* Lexi's sleep schedule was all screwed up, and she would sleep for only a few minutes at a time both day and night. It turned out it was many months before they saw her. She doesn't remember anything from the week before the crash to mid-July, so their visit probably wouldn't have triggered any anxiety for Lexi. However, I was being the Momma Bear and didn't want there to be any setbacks. I had sent them some photos I had taken of both girls together.

Lexi's dad, Keith, arrived from Arizona. I had not seen him since our son Marshall's graduation in 2012. He had health issues and apparently, they had worsened. It was obvious he wasn't going to be of any significant help.

Lexi sat up for three hours in bed that day and had been breathing on her own for 34 hours. This was a huge improvement, and I was incredibly happy with every little thing she did. I found it astonishing how we take our health and body functions for granted. Every step she made was a huge step in the right direction.

Because she was doing better, they were hoping to do arm surgery that day. I was hoping she wouldn't get bumped again. The restaurant where Lexi worked had been offering to bring us food. I figured this would be a good night with the entire family there waiting for her surgery. They brought enough food that we fed all the nurses on the sixth floor plus all the other patients' families. Lexi had been a hostess there, but had given her two-weeks' notice in order to be a lifeguard over the summer. She was supposed to work only another week. In spite of all that, they also did a fundraiser for her later that summer.

Guess what? The doctors finally did her surgery. It probably didn't hurt that my friend had contacted the president. It was pushed back from 5:30 to 7:30 p.m., and they finally took her down about 10:30 p.m. Ray and I walked to the operating room with her. I was freaking out that the doctor had been working all day and would be too tired, but the nurses told me it's what they do, and they assured me he was an excellent doctor. The orthopedic physician's assistant had also told me that he was the doctor she would want if it were her daughter getting surgery.

I was completely exhausted by the time they wheeled her down. With my ex-husband staying at my son's, I had planned to spend the night at a friend's house close to the hospital. I left Ray, Marshall, and Lexi's dad at the hospital and went to get some sleep. I was unsuccessfully trying to sleep when the doctor called me at midnight from the operating room. When he explained her elbow was "liquefied," I almost threw up. He was going to have to fuse it in place, meaning she won't be able to straighten or bend it. Ray and Marshall stayed at the hospital until the surgery was over and she was back in her room. Ray arrived at our friend's house about one a.m. We left our friend's house before six a.m. to head back to the hospital.

While my world was a small hospital room, life went on for others. The girls' friends, the high school, and our entire community were reeling from the loss. With the crash happening four weeks before graduation, their friends wanted seats to be left empty for the girls during graduation. It caused a big uproar. The district didn't want to set a precedent, but their friends gained lots of media attention and even involved the mayor. I could see both sides. The Davises really wanted it, and I could understand why. The high school principal came to see me at the hospital to tell me the seats the girls should have sat in would be left empty during the graduation ceremony.

Day 16: June 3: Saturday – Prom Day

I talked to the arm surgeon who explained that Lexi's arm was in pieces. Her forearm was intact, but her elbow joint was shattered, and the bottom of her humorous was destroyed. There was not enough bone left to anchor a joint. He put in a total of nine pins and an L-shaped plate in her arm. It was fused at 60 degrees. He didn't know if she would be able to turn her hand. He took the bone fragments, moved them together, and put in special growth sheets to help her bone grow. She wouldn't need a sling once it was healed. The good news is it was her left hand and she is right-handed. The doctor has been a trauma surgeon for 30 years and had never had to fuse an elbow. Since then, many, many doctors all over the country have looked at her x-rays and have never seen such trauma. If she hadn't been reaching back petting the puppy, her arm may have been broken, but it would have been fixable. I've spent many hours wishing things would be different.

This was the day of the prom for her high school. She had looked forward to this day for months. We had purchased a very expensive dress. It was so expensive I made her pay for part of it. She had appointments for her hair and make-up that I had to cancel. Lexi had organized a group of about 30 with a party bus and dinner reservations. The group went to the restaurant as they had planned. The restaurant had flowers and notes for both families. It was very touching and meant so much to us. Her friends brought us the cards and flowers. I found out much later that Abby's date and Lexi's date went to prom together. Abby and Lexi were voted prom queens. Under any other circumstances, they both would have loved that. How they would have laughed.

Day 18: Monday, June 5

> **Notes from doctor's rounds:**
> She had no acute events overnight, her legs are a 1 out of 5, her left pupil remains fixed. They are giving her Tylenol every 4 hours for her fever. Her pain was better controlled today; she had a dip in her blood pressure overnight. Her last temp was 102, but she was averaging 100.3, her white blood cell was 10.6 but cultures were negative. They plan to downsize her trach. Because her heart rate is going up, I asked if her drugs should be switched.

Because Lexi was sitting up and reaching for things, she was wearing the first of many mitts to prevent her from pulling out tubes or IVs. It was exhausting being with her because she had to be watched every second. In the past, I could always tell when Lexi was truly sick because she wanted me to sit with her and rub her back. So constantly during this time when I could reach her back, I would rub it. We also massaged her feet. Ray gives great foot massages, so he was on foot duty. We used the scented oils to stimulate her sense of smell.

The Shepherd Center's admittance woman flew in to see us. We spoke to her and she saw Lexi and met with her doctors. She was our key to a miracle. I hoped we had done everything right.

That evening Lexi reached for Vern, her stepbrother, and hugged me. That hug *was amazing.*

Marshall had the idea of giving Lexi a phone, hoping she would text us. Like any other teenager, before the crash she would text all the time. When she saw the phone, she grabbed for it and pushed buttons but didn't text us anything. We were disappointed that it didn't work, but it was worth a try.

We were hoping it was the trach that was not allowing her to talk. They told us they would downsize her trach to see if it would help her talk.

My notes that day:
Both Ray and I are barely functioning; our brains are a fog. I talked to the Shepherd Center admittance woman, and she said it would be okay if we rotate shifts once Lexi's at Shepherd Center in Atlanta. I am exploring options, so I can try to keep my job while having someone with her in Atlanta. The admittance person told me she knows other families who have done that. My thought process was we would go in two-week shifts, and I am planning a schedule for who will be there. My sister Laura has been incredible, she wants to help in Atlanta. Olga and Jamie both offered to fly out from California to be there for a week at a time. Her dad wants to help also, but I don't know if he is physically able.

Day 19: Tuesday, June 6

Notes from doctor's rounds:
Day 6 of trach. She is opening her right eye spontaneously, but left pupil is fixed. She has not been on the ventilator since the third. Her heart rate is tacky; blood pressure is 122/75. Temp is 99; she is on a cooling blanket. They will switch out trach tomorrow to smaller size. They may have to put in a PEG tube for feeding tomorrow, which would be another surgery. She is good enough to transfer out of the burn trauma unit.

NOTE: A PEG is flexible feeding tube that is placed through the abdominal wall and into the stomach. PEG allows nutrition, fluids and or medications to be put directly into the stomach, bypassing the mouth and esophagus. I was so happy in the end that she didn't need a PEG. I wanted to avoid extra surgeries at all costs. Every incision is an opportunity for an infection, and *I wanted to avoid infections.*

This is what we had been waiting for. Now that she could travel, my work ramped up to try to get her into Shepherd Center in Atlanta as soon as possible. We were happy that she wasn't critical anymore and could be in the step-down unit.

When the physical therapist asked her to point at Mom, she pointed to me—a huge sign that her mind was there and she knew who people were.

Before she was transferred out of ICU, our attorney came over to see Lexi. He told me many months later she looked like a broken china doll and he was worried about her future.

Chapter 7

Step Down Unit: The Next Step After ICU

This was the next step that we had been waiting for. She was *out of ICU*.

When I texted our other children to give them the new room number and directions, Marshall texted back and said we were close to the "nicer" bathrooms, and Ellie responded, "Oh thank the Lord. LOL!"

Lexi was very agitated. She wanted to sit up and was trying to climb out of the bed with her right leg. Her left side wasn't moving yet. She brushed her hair on her own and waved to her sister, Ellie, both huge steps.

The ICU nurses were right about step-down: it was hard to get any help and we definitely needed to have someone with her at all times. I spent the first night. Lexi was very restless and didn't sleep more than a few hours. She was pulling herself up and rocking back and forth. She patted me on the back. She gave a thumb's up and waved her hand back and forth when asked how she feels. This means she understood us when we asked her questions, and that was HUGE! She had peed and pooped, which may have been part of her restlessness. It was hard to get someone to come in and clean her up. The room was even smaller than the ICU. Again, we weren't allowed to use the bathroom in her room. I didn't understand this because she wasn't using it, so yeah, now we had a new area of dirty bathrooms to use.

When we were in ICU, no one could get in without our permission; in step-down it's different as the unit isn't locked down. Her friends had respected my request not to come to the hospital, but I still didn't want anyone coming into her room. The nurses put up a sign on her door that said, "No visitors." It wasn't too much of an issue—someone from the family was with her all day, every day.

I sent out this text to some of her friends: She is out of ICU! The therapists came in and they had to hold her up, but she brushed her hair. It is fantastic how things have changed in three weeks. Keep up the prayers that we will soon be in Atlanta at rehab. They are checking on bed availability now.

Day 20: Wednesday June 7

I was thinking, "we must get out of here; we can't do a week". I had spent the first night with her and it was a horrible ordeal. We were both exhausted, and it was impossible to find anyone if you have a real need. I called the Shepherd Center admittance woman and left a message, begging her to get us to Shepherd. I told her I would donate any amount of money . . . please get us there.

It was amazing the connections we had to people who had been at Shepherd Center. Terri Davis had a co-worker, Ella, whose son-in-law was at Shepherd because he had been hit by a drunk driver and was paralyzed. When Ella and I connected, she told me how excellent Sheherd Center was, and to know we could get some sleep once we get there as the staff is great. I was pulling every string I could to get us there as soon as possible.

This was not a good time to have changed jobs for lots of reasons, but a major one was insurance. I had my old company's insurance through June 1st; then I added Cobra at over $900 a month, covering us through July 1 just in case there were any issues getting my new insurance. My new employer's insurance was scheduled to start June 1, and we had added Ray's work insurance, as well as Ray's military insurance from serving 22 years in the Navy, both effective the day we were married. Trying to coordinate all the details with Shepherd Center was a huge pain. Before you get to any rehabilitation hospital, they want to make sure you have insurance. I wanted to make sure they knew we had plenty of insurance.

I was moving Lexi's legs the way the physical therapist had showed me and she grimaced. I asked her if her leg hurt and she shook her head yes. It could have been because she hadn't moved them in a long time, but it also could be a broken bone. I made a note to ask the doctor to do an x-ray if they hadn't done one already.

I was used to rounds in the ICU with about ten medical professionals. In step-down we had only one or two doctors coming in. Neither of the doctors were the same as in the ICU, so I didn't have any relationship with them. Another difference in step-down.

Notes from doctor's rounds:
Temp 97.3 had a restless night, she can swallow but her jaw is clenched. She took some liquid, but we need to watch her, so she doesn't aspirate. She took liquid so she won't need a PEG

inserted to feed her.

She didn't sleep at all last night. She was a mess, and so was I.

So many of her friends were texting me asking to see her before we left for Atlanta, but I had to limit it to just a few friends. Her friend, Summer was the first one I allowed to see her. Summer was living in Florida, working and going to school down there. When she found out about the crash, she drove straight to Virginia, about a 12-hour drive. The girls had met a few years earlier at Young Life, a Christian club for teens. Summer is older, so I was hoping she could handle it. Summer was a godsend on our journey. Katie and her mom, Kristen, also came up in the afternoon. I have a heart-breaking photo of Lexi and Katie. They are holding hands and Lexi is looking off into space. I reminded Katie not to say anything about Abby. This was the first of many times I would tell her friends *not to mention Abby*.

Lexi ate some applesauce. Hallelujah. Praise the Lord.

Day 21: Thursday, June 8

I stayed the night, and once again, it was a total nightmare. I noted: "I can't handle this." They had to re-do her IV, and her veins were blown. This was an ongoing issue. She had only the one good arm, and she was poked and prodded many times a day. This would go on for many months.

At 5:29 a.m., she gave me lots of kisses. Physical therapy came in to evaluate her and see what she could move. She kicked her right leg, but she couldn't move her left leg. They tried to have her put on her socks, but she couldn't. They helped her put on lip moisturizer. They asked her to wash her face and she did it. She was squeezing a hand when asked and giving thumbs up and the peace sign.

She was smiling and sticking out her tongue. Every little step was a giant leap forward and I was so happy with the slightest progress. I remember they told us she was like an infant; the learning would go faster, but she would have to relearn virtually everything.

Finally, she was sleeping. Every time she slept, they came in to do something, Grrrrr. The step-down unit certainly was not the ICU. I couldn't leave her alone in there. She was more alert, and today she pulled herself up so I could rub her back. Her back was not bruised. She brushed her hair and kissed my hand. Fantastic! I was crying tears of joy for a change.

The Shepherd Center called, and we were moved up a day, so we should be going to Atlanta on Monday, although I was hoping they moved it up more. I was so excited to get to Atlanta so they could really start her rehabilitation.

Ray and I had to get my military ID and get Lexi added onto his insurance. Marshall and Vern stayed with Lexi. We didn't have correct paperwork the first time, and we had to run home and get it. As with any government organization, it took longer than we had planned. It was about five hours before we returned to the hospital, despite our best efforts. Both boys were exhausted and said they didn't know how we were doing this. Vern said it was like being with a one-year-old that couldn't speak. That was a good analogy, but it was like being with a one-year-old in an 18-year old's body.

Day 22: Friday, June 9

Lexi talked . . . and I have never been happier to hear her voice. I saw her moving her lips, and I had the respiratory therapist put in a smaller unit in her trach, allowing her to finally be able to speak. She said hello and knew her name. I said, "I love you." She asked, "What does that mean?"

When I told her again, "I love you," she said, "So?" She told me her right shin hurt. She thought I was Melanie or Marshall. She grabbed her toothbrush and tried to brush her teeth. When I asked if she wanted Emma to come see her, she said, "Maybe." She was counting but started at 16; she thinks it's 1940 something. Today when the nurse was helping her, she said, " I want to go to your house." The nurse replied, "You need to get stronger," and Lexi said, "I am strong." When her brother told her to "take a cat nap," she said, "I need to take a human nap." We all laughed at that—it was great to laugh again.

Lexi talking was a huge milestone and an immense relief. We didn't know if she would be able to ever talk again. It depends what side of your brain is injured and exactly what is damaged.

She told the physical therapist, "I don't like this place." She told me, "We need to leave." She said, "I'm confused."

I had her on-line music account set up right after the crash, allowing me to play her music while she was in the ICU. We played it as much as we could as music can stimulate the mind. Today she sang along to "Stand by Me"— which will always be my favorite song.

She ate some pancakes and applesauce. I brought her a Frappuccino, which made her happy because she *loves her coffee*. Her IV was out; one less tube was fantastic!

Her friend Ashley came to see her and brought her a soft blanket to take along to the Shepherd Center. Ashley was going to college in the south, so she and her mom would be able to stop by Atlanta to see us.

Liz, the crash witness who was a nurse, came by the hospital to see her too. As I hugged her hard, tears were streaming down my face. She helped save my baby. She confirmed what Lexi's sister Ellie had thought, Lexi's hair had flown over her face in the crash and protected it from damage. I am so grateful that her face wasn't hurt. Lexi was very conscious of her looks and it would make her recovery easier if she looked the same. I saw the admitting doctor in the hallway ahead of me and flagged her down. She came to Lexi's room to see her and told me she was a miracle, saying, "It was touch and go for a while." That was so hard for all of us to hear.

Below is an email I received from the AP Biology teacher, a class Lexi and Abby were in together. She was also a chaperone on the European trip the girls went on a few years earlier and knew both girls well. Subject: AP Biology with Abby and Lexi:

Good Afternoon,

I wanted to share with you some letters that my third and fourth block AP Biology family wanted to share. This is being sent to both families. We invite you to view the letters we wrote on Google docs earlier this week. We have taken time to grieve, gather, console, and remember our girls, but moving forward is never easy. We love and miss them both so much. Our thoughts and many prayers are with you every day. I hope you feel some comfort by the actions of our youth, Abby and Lexi's closest friends especially. They have found great strength in one another, and to be their teacher, I am honored and privileged to have helped guide them through this loss. I know what we feel pales in comparison to how your lives have changed forever. Please know I will never forget your girls—from their smiles and their laughs, to their dedication and hard work I observed every day.

> We are a family all year long. We laugh and learn and cry and complain with one another every day. Mostly, we laugh. We form friendships that last a lifetime.
>
> Abby and Lexi are magnificent girls. Our hearts love differently because of them, and I am so grateful to have taught them and to have traveled with them. I have unique memories of both girls, and I will never forget them. From crowding into a European hotel room at night sharing cookies and brownies, to picking up mobile orders at a coffee shop's drive-thru during my lunch. Your girls have a fire within them that all the blonde hair masked. They are tough mentally and physically—incredible. I have great faith that Lexi can do this. I wish her all the best for her continued recovery and healing. I pray that you feel the outpouring of love and support from our community for a long time. May God bless your families.

This was just one of many emails or letters I received about both girls' impact on others. I was so moved by all the stories. I always knew how special Lexi was, but to hear how she had impacted others was wonderful. Another reason for her to fight to survive. I responded back early the next morning, thanking the teacher and students.

Day 23: Saturday, June 10

When I woke up at two a.m. I realized I was not going to wake up from this nightmare. This was real, and it was happening to us. Since the crash I usually woke up at three a.m. I called it my witching hour. After that I rarely went back to sleep. I was so tired and stressed out it was surprising I haven't gotten into a car accident or fallen down the stairs.

It was another long day at the hospital. At 10:40a.m. Lexi was in a chair napping. Today they removed her trach. Lexi was eating solid foods after a day of only liquids. I brought her favorite foods from outside the hospital including chicken nuggets, fries, and a shake.

The plan was to leave Monday morning for Atlanta, heading to one of the best rehab centers in the country. We were very lucky that she was accepted there.

Graduation was coming up, and the principal reached out to me about getting her diploma. Ray and I would be in Atlanta with her, so Marshall planned to go to the ceremony to accept it.

This was the first time I had been home by myself since the crash, because Ray was staying at the hospital with Lexi. It was hard for a very long time to be home, especially alone. I did plenty of crying when Ray was there, but when I was alone, I bawled. It was hard to go into Lexi's room. That day I found a gratitude list she had made. I had been encouraging her to keep a gratitude journal, to keep in mind how lucky she was. It is hard being a teenager, and I wanted her to keep things in perspective. She listed what she was grateful for; I sent the list to some of her friends. One of the things on the list was Abby. Oh God, that was like a kick in the gut. How were we going to tell her Abby was gone?

Day 24: Sunday, June 11

Ray stayed with her overnight and said it was awful. She hardly slept and was constantly doing sit ups all hours of day and night. He stopped counting after 70 in a row. I was at home but couldn't sleep, arriving at the hospital early.

At six a.m. the doctor came in and said her heart rate was "tacky," which meant her heart was beating too fast.

I played her music for her, which at times calmed her down. She was pulling on her trach bandage, and we had to constantly watch her. She continued to constantly pull herself up, it might be a way to self-sooth by rocking like a baby does. It was a good thing she had such rock-hard abs before the crash. She was peeing, which was good. The diapers were horrible, allowing much of it to run onto the floor.

When she awoke at eight a.m., I fed her and Ray went home to sleep. He told me she had choked on pasta last night. She choked on a pancake this morning and I had to call for help. Again, getting help was almost impossible. The nurses covered her trach hole when she ate, which made a difference, but it was scary. She was back to sleep at 8:40 a.m. That was when I stood outside her room and wouldn't let anyone come in to take her vitals. I didn't want them to wake her for something that could be done later. I know they were trying to do their job, but she needed sleep to heal. Watch out for Mamma Bear. I found out afterwards, and it is in my "things to know" list, but you can ask for a "do not disturb" order.

Today should have been her graduation party and last Friday Ray and I should have been at the Neil Diamond concert together.

I hated to see my daughter like this. Her friend Emma came to see her. Emma told me how school had been very sad. I had sent a text about Lexi talking, and Kristen and Katie were sitting outside a coffee shop when they saw it. They cried with happiness.

Lexi's friend Anita came to the hospital and brought her favorite coffee. Lexi was in a chair, and we rolled her to the windows. She had trouble sitting up on her own and needed to be propped up. She was biting at everything, including us. Lexi asked me if I would help her succeed. I cried and said of course I would. I had been helping her succeed for 18 years; I wasn't going to stop now. We pushed her in the chair around the nurse's station in the hospital until she finally fell asleep at 11 a.m.

The feeling of powerlessness was tearing apart my heart.

Chapter 8

A Private Jet

"Even miracles take a little time."
– Pablo Casals

Day 25: Monday, June 12

We were leaving. I had never been this happy to be going
anywhere. Lexi had slept only four hours all night. Yes, I
kept track. They gave her anti-anxiety meds and something to sleep, but it didn't work. She moved her left leg
sideways on her own. Her left arm is causing her a lot of
pain, especially when she has to roll on it.

Right before we left the last of her friends came. Emily,
who is like my second daughter. Lexi almost cried when
she saw her. Lexi spelled her name for Emily. I tried to
prepare her friends before they saw her, but nothing could
prepare them for this, especially at age 18. After leaving
her room, Emily and I stood in the hallway and held each
other and cried. Her dad and Marshall were there to say
good-bye. Luckily, both Ray and I could fly on the plane,
and take along a small suitcase.

We left the hospital a little after nine a.m. Lexi was
super-agitated in the ambulance, biting the ace bandage
around her IV and slapping me. She finally fell asleep for
maybe 10 minutes. For some reason, the driver went the
long way through the neighborhoods. I couldn't figure
out why he was taking the long way. Ray and I were too

afraid and scared to say anything, but we knew the fastest way to the airport, and he didn't take it. My anxiety was off the charts.

We finally arrived at the airport for private planes. We met the crew and loaded her onto the plane. Lexi was strapped into a stretcher. I took a lot of photos of the plane so she could see it later. In normal circumstances she would have been thrilled. The plane was very small and crowded. Ray sat in front and I sat next to her and a nurse was behind us. Lexi was super agitated, flailing and fighting. It was horrible. For brain injury patient's stimulation is hard, and this was a lot of stimulation. She was pulling up and hitting me and biting. Finally, at 11:15 the nurse gave her something to knock her out and it worked. I remember the other nurse asked how much sedative he had given her and based on his reaction I thought it might be too much. I was scared. What if she didn't wake up after all this?

This is what I wrote on the plane: "I have never been this exhausted. In the early days someone told me I was going to need more paper for this notebook, and they were right. I'm happy to be going to Shepherd Center. Ray is my rock—and I couldn't do this without him."

When we landed, she was still sedated, which made the ambulance ride better. We arrived at Shepherd Center at 2:15 p.m. They rolled her into the building and up to the fourth floor. She was put in ICU because they didn't have a bed for her. Later, the doctor told me she approved our trip even though a bed wasn't available because I was so frantic. I will always be grateful for that.

While they were getting her settled in, Ray and I ate some food at the hospital cafeteria. It wasn't great, but it was food.

That night she asked Ray and me to help her go home. I was in the depths of hell: that was how I felt as they put in another IV. I hated to see her in such pain. I wished with all my heart it were me and not her in that hospital bed.

Chapter 9

Shepherd Center at Last

*"When you have a trauma,
At first it is minute by minute,
Then it will be hour by hour,
Finally, it will go to day-to-day, and then
Eventually, it will be month by month."*

— The doctors at Shepherd Center

Wow, this place was impressive. It was huge and they had all kinds of awards in the hallway and individuals' stories of success. They settled her into a bed in the ICU. We were told we couldn't give her anything to eat or drink until the speech therapist evaluated her. Her temp was 101.5. They did an ultrasound to check her for blood clots.

At three p.m. I was playing music and she was singing along to "Stand by Me" again. At 3:30 p.m., they came to evaluate her to see if she could swallow. They didn't do this at the *first* trauma center and that was why she was choking on food. This place knew what they were doing. They said she was the best swallower they had seen all day, making me proud. Her tongue muscle was weak, but once she eats, they told us that will come back. They explained that different foods would help her muscles develop. They gave her medicine (amantadine) to help her brain neurons connect. She asked us to help her get home, and we told her we were. She said, "Get Ashley," her friend. When I texted Ashley, she texted back and said she would be one of the first people to help her break out when she was ready.

We ran over and checked into an apartment in the building next door. You walk through a parking garage to get there. It was nothing fancy, but it was wonderful to be that close to Lexi's hospital room. I would do that walk many times a day for months to come.

Day 26: Tuesday, June 13

When I arrived early this morning, they told me she pulled out the IV while she was getting blood and blood spewed all over the room. Thank God we weren't there. They put an IV in her foot so she couldn't reach it. They checked for a sepsis infection. She was on IV fluids the previous night. She hadn't slept much. They were going to try to change her medication to see if she would start sleeping better.

Her main doctor came in and said she was doing great compared to what was on her chart, and for it being so soon after her injury. Ray started to cry. She had an infection, and they couldn't understand why, so she stayed another night in the ICU.

They fitted her for a wheelchair that allowed her to sit up for an hour at a time. The chair would tilt back so we could lessen the pressure for one minute every fifteen minutes. I asked her where it hurt and she said, "Everywhere." She said, "I'm so happy for you." When I asked her why, she said, "Marriage."

My notes at 7 a.m.:
A month ago was my engagement party and birthday. I really lost it last night. She needed a blood transfusion, and they had to put in a bigger IV because they have such a hard time finding a vein. The risks of the transfusion and everything else just got to me. Ray had me leave and go back to the room. It is very

> hard for me to see her in such pain. She asked
> me to help her go home. The staff here is great;
> I'm very happy she is here. They put a catheter
> in last night.

We moved into the apartment, which was like a budget motel, but it wasn't costing us anything (at least directly). It had linoleum floors and basic furniture, but we had a kitchen, with a dishwasher. The pillows were awful, and I planned to get better ones. The twin beds were attached to the wall so we couldn't even push them together. This was the suckiest honeymoon on the face of the earth!

Shepherd Center has many wonderful volunteers. One drove me to get pillows and other things we needed. We discovered a grocery store that offered delivery service, and we ordered food and heavy things such as water bottles. This store even brought the stuff up to the apartment and helped Ray put it away. Because we had flown in, we didn't have a car, but enough things were close that we didn't need it.

The first morning we were there, I walked to a coffee shop, and Ray stayed with Lexi. We were told it was close, but it was a mile away. When I was walking it was strange being outside. By the time I arrived I was tired, not having walked that far since before the crash. About a week later they opened a new coffee shop right across the street. Not having a car, we continued to walk a lot. I felt like I was always running back and forth to the room or running to pick up food or coffee.

That night, Ella, Terri Davis's co-worker, brought us dinner. She had been at Shepherd Center for a while caring for her son-in-law. She told me about a house they rented and that's why I originally thought we would need long-term housing—thinking we would be here for a year because they told us that was the golden time for rehab.

Turns out I was wrong. That night I wrote:

- Good things:
    - We're here
    - Have housing
    - Lexi swallows well
    - Ella
- Bad things:
    - We're here
    - Blood
    - Agitation
    - Twin beds
    - Cafeteria in hospital

Day 27: Wednesday, June 14

When I walked off the elevator that morning a nurse said, "It's a great day to be alive." Amen to that. I must have had that shell-shocked look of a new arrival. When I arrived at seven a.m., Lexi was asleep. Later, they gave her a sponge bath, only the second one after the crash. She was in a lot of pain. She kept biting, and today, left a mark on my arm.

They had different meetings for the Shepherd families. We were encouraged to attend family orientation the first week so we would know what to expect on this journey.

Ray went and here are his notes:
They will train us before we are able to help with anything. They encourage active participation. Watch overstimulation as it adversely

affects rest. Write down questions before medical meeting. There will be a goal-setting session. Do not take patients to apartments. Chain of command—use if needed.

There are out-of-bed times and back-to-bed times. She will build core strength but will be tired. Fill out home-modification form as they will use this information to help us with any modifications that need to be made before she comes home.

They moved her out of ICU and into a beautiful corner room, much larger than we had before, with lots of windows and light. There were two chairs, one that reclined, but it was incredibly uncomfortable. She was in a lot of pain, which is very hard to watch, and I was beyond exhausted. Ray came into the room and fell asleep with a cookie in his mouth.

The physical therapists helped her put on her own clothes today, the first time since the crash.

I received a request from the fatal crash investigator that he wanted to talk to her to see what she remembered from the day of the crash; I didn't reply. Lexi wouldn't remember anything for a long time, and still doesn't recall the crash.

Day 28: Thursday, June 15

Lexi slept only four hours total and was awake from one a.m. to five a.m. but she was asleep when I came in. Some family members stay in the hospital room. I couldn't do that because I needed my sleep under the best of circumstances. They charted her sleep by checking on her every hour. Every morning when I arrived if she was awake, I would tell her good morning and give her a hug and a kiss, then I would check the chart. Her body clock was all off-kilter. ICU delirium was to blame for her upset sleep pattern. She needed to sleep for her brain to heal so it was very upsetting to me. I would try to get to the hospital before the nurses shift change at seven a.m. so I could talk to the night nurse to see how she did the previous night.

Lexi had a shower. Earlier I had run across the street to the drug store and bought her good-smelling body wash, shampoo and conditioner. She loves things that smell good like any girl, but I wanted her showers to be extra special and I hoped the scent would help stimulate her brain. The therapists said I could wash her hair. How I treasure the memory of those showers. She couldn't wash her hair due to her arm. Now I realize why she goes through so much shampoo and conditioner: it takes a lot to wash all that long hair. The occupational therapists would have her wash whatever she could. They would coach her to put body wash on a loofa and cue her to wash her body parts as she could. It was hard for me because I wanted to jump in and help her, but they had me back off. Lexi is extremely modest, and luckily, she doesn't remember all of us being in the bathroom when she showered. Her hair would get tangled because she was in bed a lot. We tried to keep it braided and that helped, but it was a constant mess. It hurt when I combed it to get the knots out, which broke my heart. At one point I said we may need to cut her hair, and she said, "You *are not* cutting my hair!"

Yesterday we met the doctor, therapists and other people who would be part of her team, and they were great.

My notes:
When eating, have her dry swallow between bites; have her focus on one thing at a time. Choices are good . . . give her choices. It is normal that she will be disoriented, so help

to reorient her. Tell her where she is and what happened in general terms. Ask her math questions, her attention span is very limited, less is more. Make sure she has downtime during therapy. Talk to her about long-term goals such as walking and going to college.

I saw this quote today by James Brady: "What is the difference between a stumbling block and a stepping stone? It's all in the way you approach it." James Brady was President Regan's Press Secretary. He was treated at Shepherd Center after he was shot during the assassination attempt on President Ronald Regan.

An outside massage therapist comes to Shepherd Center and I pampered myself with a much-needed chair massage today. The masseuse suffered a brain injury in an auto accident when he was young. It was before Shepherd Center was open, so he wasn't treated there. By volunteering once a week to help the families, he was giving back. I was most touched by his story.

She was in so much pain; we needed to monitor it because they were giving her opioids. I was terrified she would become addicted. I have heard many horror stories about the opioid epidemic.

Now out of ICU, she could work with the therapists. At lunch she worked with a speech therapist and ate a grilled cheese sandwich. The speech therapist was helping her to re-learn how to swallow. She was able to hold the sandwich and feed herself. We encouraged her to take dry swallows between bites like we had been told. She didn't remember how to eat; this is typical of a brain injury. In physical therapy she kicked a ball and took steps. Her schedule was full, but rest time was built in. She didn't rest much during downtime even though she was exhausted.

Her trach hole was not healing well, and we were told

she may need surgery to close the hole. We would see a special doctor for that.

The orthopedic surgeon talked to Ray and me today about her arm. He said that fusion should be a last resort. He asked us if they had mentioned amputation; we were aghast and said, "NO!" He wanted to do a CAT scan and see if he could do surgery to give her movement. He gave us hope, but also scared the crap out of us with the talk of amputation.

I did an interview with our local newspaper. I wanted to talk to the press to express my gratitude for the over-whelming support from the community. I remember being in the waiting room of the ICU unit and talking to the reporter by phone about what we had been going through. I had to be careful not to say too much about her medical condition due to legal reasons.

Day 29: June 16th Graduation Day

My notes:
Today on her graduation day I wake up at a rehab hospital in Atlanta. I am eternally grateful that she is alive and that she is here in one of the top places in the country. However, I continue to grieve for what should have been. As I look at the photos of her friends graduating, I am both proud of them and sorry she won't be able to walk across the stage tonight with the kids she has spent her life with.

The doctors say she won't remember this part of her recovery—and for that I am grateful. She is in a lot of pain.

Her friend, Summer, is coming for a while today. She took a job for the summer in Tennessee and will be close to Atlanta. I hope that will

cheer up Lexi. Ray will go home on Sunday for
a few days.

That morning I sent a text to her friends that said, "As
you guys walk across the stage tonight, cherish every step
you take. Lexi was very excited to graduate, and I know she
is so proud of you all. She will be with you there in spirit.
Be careful tonight, as I told Lexi over a month ago, this is a
dangerous time, and someone almost always dies around
this time of year. Congratulations to the class of 2017!"
They all responded with how proud they were of Lexi for
the progress she was making and how much they love her.

My notes:
She didn't sleep well. The nurses changed
her shirt. Her arm hurts when they change
her shirt or have her move it at all. We met
with the speech therapist, and here is what I
wrote: Provide what she can do, don't tell her
"No." Get her a squishy ball for her hands, play
games with her, Tick-tack-toe, Uno, etc. She
suggested when we are playing Tick-tack-toe to
say, "You go," ask her, "Whose turn is it?" Give
her time before you help her, she is processing
things slower than before. Say, "Good try," ask,
"Where do you need to go to block me?" Direct
her to "look for missing spot."
When we are playing Uno, ask her, "What
color? What number? Hold up two cards and
ask her which is #8? Say, "Nice job," and tell
her when we were going to switch gears. They
also suggested a few more tips: Ask her to name
four colors, give her three words and ask her to
repeat them. She keeps pulling at her bandages,
so we should tell her, "Put your hand down in

your lap." They told us to do these things for 15 minutes and give her a break.

Day 30: Saturday, June 17

Last night many friends sent me photos of her name up on the Jumbotron as well as videos of my son accepting her diploma. The Davises were on TV getting Abby's diploma. A lot of the kids had ribbons for the girls or were wearing buttons with the girls' photo. It was incredibly sad. My son's face was filled with such sadness. What should have been a highlight of everyone's lives was overlaid with sadness due to a jerk who was driving drunk and drugged on a beautiful Friday afternoon.

I almost always arrived at her hospital room by six or seven a.m. I wasn't sleeping much anyway. Curtis, her nurse last night, told me she had slept the most since she had arrived. He noticed she was restless when she slept, I had noticed that, too. At seven a.m. she was in such pain she was crying. I was hoping they would be in soon with her pain meds as I can't get anyone to come in during shift change.

She fed herself scrambled eggs, which was important because I had been feeding her them before. She hates eggs . . . I mean really hates eggs. The fact that she was eating them told me how out of it she was. However, eggs are a great source of protein, and she hadn't eaten for a long time. She had lost a ton of weight.

Being at Shepherd Center made me realize how lucky she was. Her neighbor was an infection risk, requiring everyone to gown up to enter his room. Many patients had helmets on because their skull had been opened due to brain swelling. Many patients were left up at the nurses' stations when therapy was over as they had no one to watch them when they were in their rooms. We would always try to smile and say hello to those patients. We met one young man when we first arrived. He had been in a motorcycle crash. He was great talking to Lexi and encouraging her. He was further along in this journey. Because his mom had to be at work, we would talk to him. When I went shopping, I asked him if he liked candy. After getting the okay from the therapist, I brought back candy bars for him.

I had found a great yoga studio that I could walk to. I needed to do something to help me get through this. Of course, I was at yoga when Lexi took a step on her own with her left leg. Her brain injury was on the right side and the right side of your brain controls the left side of your body. We had numerous x-rays done of her leg to make sure it wasn't broken because she couldn't move and she was in so much pain for so long.

She had an MRI to check her heart. She has had so many MRIs and x-rays; I worry about her future health, but there was nothing I could do. *We had to take care of the here and now.*

Day 31: Sunday, June 18

Lexi slept only two hours last night. I was there before seven a.m., and she slept from seven to 7:30 a.m. Then she wouldn't eat breakfast, saying she was too tired. Sunday is a rest day with no therapy at Shepherd. I wanted her to take advantage of this downtime and sleep. I walked over to get coffee at nine and she was still asleep when I returned. I was delighted any time she slept.

Shepherd had a lift to get patients out of bed. It was quite a contraption to get Lexi strapped into it every time she needed to get in and out of bed. Until they taught us how to do it, we needed a nurse's help. Lexi was in a wheelchair and I had to learn how to help her if she had a seizure. Once I was signed off on the seizure lesson, I was able to take her off the floor. I took her down to the "secret garden," which isn't secret at all, but beautiful. It was the first time she had been outside, except for the flight. In less than a minute she said, "Too much." We headed back to her room because she was over-stimulated.

Yesterday she was mad at me, so I left her with Ray. He left this morning, and now I will be alone with her. It would be much harder having just me. I didn't want to leave her for too long so I ran (and I mean ran) across the street to an upscale grocery store. They had a roasted chicken with two sides and four corn muffins for only $13. I selected total comfort food for dinner—chicken and mashed potatoes and mac and cheese—and she ate everything I gave her.

She texted a few friends using my phone.

Day 32: Monday, June 19

One month ago was the crash. It was exhausting being there by myself. Lexi slept only about four hours and needed lots of medicine because she was in such excruciating pain. She kept throwing her good leg over the bed and trying to crawl out, which set off the bed alarm. She wanted out so badly. They had to put up a sideboard; now she couldn't get her leg over and the bed alarm would stop going off. The nurses had to tie her down to the bed and she had to wear a glove when we weren't there to prevent her from pulling on everything or setting off the alarm. When we were with her, we removed the glove, but sometimes it was too much even for us. She even used her teeth to pull off the glove, meaning we had to be watching her every second. Seeing her in such pain—and not being able to help any more than I could—was beyond the worst feeling I have ever had. As a parent, I have always tried to protect my kids from pain. I felt helpless and have never been this tired in my life.

Yesterday, she said she wanted to be in her own bed. I wanted that, too. I can't help but think about when I kissed her goodbye the morning I left for Dallas and she was peacefully sleeping. Will I see that again? She told me I was pathetic because I was tired and wanted to go back to the apartment and sleep.

The nurses were helping her get dressed in her own clothes. This gave her a little control and helped her feel normal. I had packed a few of her clothes before we left home. I grabbed things that were in the top of her drawers. She told me she didn't wear any of the things I brought. I asked her why she had kept them.

A month after the crash, a bruise by her left ear remained, but the others have healed. Her legs had been extremely bruised, and took this entire time to heal. Given how they looked I was amazed she had not broken her legs.

My notes:

12:50 p.m., and I am waiting for the doctor to come in because her trach isn't healing the way it should. They are going to scope her throat to make sure there isn't any permanent damage due to the tube being in for so long. That was one of the reasons they wanted to do the trach sooner, but she wasn't stable enough.

We found out she has endocarditis on her heart, which is bacteria from the sepsis infection she was subjected to in the ICU. They put her on IV antibiotics a few days ago that she'll take for at least four weeks. In addition to all the other doctors, she now has a cardiologist. They will keep an eye on her white blood count (yay, more needle sticks in her body), and do

> an echocardiogram at the end of the antibiotics
> to make sure there is no permanent damage.
> *It seems like we take two steps forward;
> then one step back.*

They made a soft cast for her arm today, and we were waiting on results of the CAT scan to see if they could do another surgery to give her movement. She was moving her left arm more, but her left hand was limp, and her fingers were quite swollen, and looked like thick sausages. I asked about a nerve scan and the doctor said they would do that later. She said, "right now, there are too many other issues." The doctors would up her sleep meds for the time being; they were trying to reset her body clock. *This nightmare never ends.*

During physical therapy, she walked with assistance halfway down a hall and she was on a stationary bike for about five minutes. She kept taking her foot off the bike pedal. This afternoon when the therapist came to get her, Lexi didn't want to get up.

I bought a smoothie for Lexi to drink after the scope. Her throat looked good, but she would need surgery to close the hole from the trach. The doctor said he could close it up so she won't have as bad of a scar, and that it would blend in with lines on her neck. As much as I hated the idea of another surgery, I knew it would help her feel better about herself.

Day 33: Tuesday, June 20

Last night, Lexi was very agitated and became progressively worse. I finally left at seven p.m. as I thought I was making it worse. Thanks to the new meds, she slept from 11 p.m. to about 6:30 a.m. She gave me a kiss when I arrived this morning . . . and I truly needed that kiss.

The soft cast seemed to make her arm more comfortable. It was hard to see her in such pain.

We were starting to get cards and her new cousins sent her flowers. I brought lots of photos of her and her friends (except Abby) that we put up all over her room. The cards decorated the window ledge, and luckily, she had a corner room with lots of windows.

My notes:
Her white blood cell count is down; that is good news. Her attention span in therapy today was two–three minutes; that is good. The catheter was removed today. Yesterday she said, "Get this out of my vagina." I loved it when I saw signs of her personality because it shows me, she is in there. I hoped she would start to pee on her own. Every little thing we take for granted is hard for her.

Our attorney suggested because she is 18 and an "adult," we should get a guardianship for her to allow me to make decisions for her. It would also allow me to make financial decisions and talk to the doctors. This hasn't been an issue in the hospital, but it may be once she gets out. This first came up with the Facebook posting when I couldn't change her password. To get a guardianship granted, she needed to be interviewed by a representative of the court called a guardian ad litem. He will determine if she could make decisions for herself. We wanted to have her interviewed before we left home, but I missed the guardian ad litem call the day before we left and was simply too tired to call him back. She talked to the guardian ad litem via conference call from her hospital room in Shepherd Center. He asked her questions such as what day it was, where she was, etc. He determined she was not able to oversee her affairs. It was obvious when you talked to her that she couldn't make major decisions. Hopefully this would only be a temporary measure.

I sent a video of Lexi as she was walking to a few of her close friends; then I texted their moms to tell them. I know the girls' friends were in such pain and I wanted the moms to know so they could help them process this. I told them to let me know if it was too upsetting. I wanted to keep them up to date, but felt I was walking a fine line. I said, "There is no guidebook for this." They texted me back that it made their daughters happy to see Lexi, and to keep sharing.

The principal at her high school emailed me that Virginia Tech had contacted them about Lexi's status. I told him, "I have not had the heart to contact Tech, and I didn't have her ID number with me. I was going to contact them when I get home the end of next week. Feel free to give them my email." It was hard for me to contact Tech because that would make me face the fact that she wouldn't be there in the fall. *I was in denial.* I finally called and they were very nice. They asked if I wanted to defer her admittance and they would keep the $400 deposit or if I wanted to withdraw her all together. I said let's defer. Then I had to decide one year or two. At this point I was worried it would be more than two years before she could go to college, if at all. But I said to do one year. They assured me we could add an extra year if we needed to. Once off the phone, I cried and cried. Earlier Ray had said he didn't think he had this many tears in him; I couldn't agree more.

Day 34: Wednesday, June 21

Lexi fell asleep at 11 pm. and was still sleeping when I arrived at 7:45 a.m. Being here was extremely hard to do alone. I felt like I walked about two miles a day back and forth to do laundry, get food, and get back to her room. I hoped today would be a good day. Last night they had to put an IV in and her veins rolled, meaning they couldn't find a good vein to put the needle in.

My Notes:
I went to new-family orientation and wrote down: It will take 7–10 days to feel comfortable with things. There are 4–5 patients for every nurse plus techs. TBI patients haven't lost their intellect; they are like a baby but will learn faster.

She was on the second floor at Shepherd Center, and when I was running errands, I mostly took the stairs because I was always in a rush. Occasionally I would take the elevator, which is when I had a few seconds where I could call my mom or a friend or just breathe. The elevator was the only place I could relax besides my few yoga classes or my massages. I hated to leave her even for a few minutes.

The neurologist came in and asked her all kinds of questions. After that we had to go to the hospital next door to get an x-ray of her left knee. Lexi said, "This is confusing."

Many brain injury patients are physically and verbally abusive and swear a lot. We experienced this with Lexi, but on the low end. While we were at Shepherd Center, a male patient fit that bill. When we first arrived, the counselor mentioned how his wife was at her wits end. Unfortunately, he was in the room next to Lexi. He would swear and scream. It was hard for everyone to witness. We all felt sorry for both him and his wife. We would talk to Lexi about how he was having a bad day when we could hear him, which was often. At one-point she said, "He is always having a bad day."

Because she was extremely active, biting out her IV and unbuckling the seat belt on her wheelchair, I had to be right with her all the time. If I ran to the apartment to do laundry, I left her up by the nurse's station where they could watch her.

She was doing well in therapy, walking some with assistance. Most parents only get to see their child learn to walk once, well I got to see it a second time. Her attention span was up to a few minutes. The last two nights they gave her meds to sleep, which was a huge help. She was sleeping better than I was.

I tried to focus on the positives. I couldn't believe it would soon be July—time was standing still for me.

Two women I have never met had t-shirts made related to the girls, raising $6,000 for each family. The outpouring of love is overwhelming.

Day 35: Thursday, June 22

Lexi had a shower yesterday and slept well. After her shower she said, "I don't want to take a bath again until I can do it myself." As she becomes more aware, she wants to shave her legs and arm pits. She can't use a razor due to the medications she is on because if she cuts herself, she wouldn't stop bleeding. We bought some cream hair removal for her.

During physical therapy this morning she was in severe pain when walking. Her right leg was very weak, but it could straighten. Her left leg was in pain, and she couldn't straighten it or put much weight on it. There were two therapists, and one sat on a stool with wheels and moved when she moved, the other held her up and helped her to move her legs. At first her steps were very slow, and she would cry in pain. It was excruciating to watch, but watch we did. We would cheer her on. Whoever stayed with her watched most therapy sessions.

We returned from therapy to find balloons and a card in her room. They were from a classmate's grandma who lives in Atlanta. Because I couldn't read the handwriting clearly, I texted her friends, and they knew who the girl was. I sent a text thanking the family. The balloons were a part of her room for a long time. I was so touched that this woman had taken the time to come by. She visited a few more times and I finally met her. Lexi was walking with assistance and I was cheering her on as always when this very kind lady walked up to me and asked me if I was Lexi's mom.

Today was our medical meeting with the doctors. The various doctors and therapists had been evaluating her, and we got to hear the treatment plan as well as find out a potential discharge date. I was quite nervous about this meeting.

I was in the meeting, while Ray and Marshall were on the phone. We had a list of eight pressing questions:

1. Opioids—get her off them

2. Pain in hip and arm

3. Arm plans?

4. Left knee x-ray

5. Signs that she's ready to leave

6. Going to the bathroom

7. Timeline for school

8. How long will we be at Shepherd Center?

My notes from this important meeting:
We were lucky she never needed brain surgery,

or a portion of her skull removed to allow her brain to swell. With a traumatic brain injury that is quite common. She did have bleeding in her brain, but it was relatively minor. The doctor explained the brain is like a bowl of gelatin, with vessels that connect to each other. She had a lot of shearing injury where those connections were broken—especially in front and on the right side of her brain. She had bleeding in different areas, which will clear up with time, but her brain will never be the same. She is on amantadine to help make new pathways. She is likely to have seizures for two years. Risk goes down but can happen up to one year after. We need to get her to ER if she has a seizure. She has a Diffuse Axonal Injury or shearing. The MRI showed a lot of shearing. Time line is 12–18 months max recovery. She is making progress. Doctor is "thrilled." We are to expect progress plateaus.

She will stay as an inpatient at Shepherd Center as long as she needs 24/7 care and a physician onsite. They will train us before we leave. The plan is she will go to Pathways, Shepherd Center's outpatient center on August 2. Pathways will be the first chapter in outpatient therapy where she will continue to get better.

She has an entire team of doctors: a throat doctor; a cardiologist; an orthopedic surgeon; and infectious disease doctor.

Her status as of the meeting: she has a high white blood count, has bacteria in her blood, and she will remain on antibiotics for several weeks. Heard a murmur in her heart;

she has endocarditis.

Mayoclinic.org describes endocarditis "as an infection of the endocardium, which is the inner lining of your heart chambers and heart valves. Endocarditis generally occurs when bacteria, fungi or other germs from another part of your body, such as your mouth, spread through your bloodstream and attach to damaged areas in your heart. If it's not treated quickly, endocarditis can damage or destroy your heart valves and can lead to life-threatening complications. Treatments for endocarditis include antibiotics and, in certain cases, surgery."

The cardiologist will repeat the echocardiogram in a few weeks. The endocarditis can be treated with antibiotics; worst case is a valve replacement. Starting antibiotics has improved her counts. The orthopedic surgeon can't do anything until the infection clears up, and then he will re-image her arm to check for healing. She is moving her fingers now but has nerve injury at bone. The doctor has shown x-rays to other orthopedists, and this is one of the most severe injuries the doctors have seen. Treatment in the hospital was appropriate and reasonable. She needs to be monitored off antibiotics for two–three weeks to make sure infection doesn't return before we can think about surgery.

They are amazed. Given her injuries, she is doing remarkably well. Seeing more personality emerge. Endurance is poor but will build with time. X-ray of knee is normal. Marshall asked about an MRI of her knee, but they want to wait a week or two.

> Catheter–she wants it out. They will add an over-the-counter medication to help her pee. Don't see it as a lasting problem, and it might be the meds. It should pass with time.
>
> They told us it is very rare that people leave here on opioids, but she needs them now for pain. They don't know of any patients who had issues afterwards. She is advancing on her diet, and they will cut back her sleeping pills as they don't want to keep her on them long.

This is our family's "new normal." We are to anticipate attention, focus, and concentration issues as well as impulse issues. Likely she won't be able to take a full load at college.

Day 36: Friday, June 23

Two years ago today we were in Europe. Lexi was there on her class trip and Ray and I were in Paris. What I would do to be able to turn back time.

Summer, Lexi's friend, was with us again. Lexi has always thought the world of her. I now knew why. The night of the crash, Summer drove back to Virginia from Florida, where she was attending college. The day after, she sent me a text about how she and Crystal, the Young Life leader, were meeting with the girls' friends to help them process losing Abby—and Lexi being critically injured. She took a job in Tennessee, allowing her to be close to Atlanta to come see Lexi. She saw Lexi on May 30th before we left for Atlanta: now she had driven five hours to see her again. She arrived last night. Lexi was happy to see her and cried. She also cried when she talked to her friend Ashley on the phone last night. She was very emotional. We tried to help her control her emotions by telling her she was doing great and to take deep breaths. With Summer here, I left to clean the apartment floors. When I came back about eight p.m. to kiss Lexi good night, she was in bed, and Summer was sitting next to her holding her hand. I said, "What are you doing?" Lexi said, "just chillin'," and smiled. It made me very happy to see a glimpse of my girl.

Lexi walked today and was in a lot of pain. I needed to push the doctor to get the MRI done.

She slept well last night and Summer stayed with her in the hospital room. They had removed the catheter but she wasn't peeing, and they had to drain her bladder; it was very painful and hard for me to watch. All I can do is hold her hand and try to distract her by asking her to count backwards. That is what I do when she is getting a shot or another awful medical procedure.

She was now sleeping between therapies. With Summer here, I went to yoga today. Ray lands tonight at eight and will be here by nine. I can't wait to see him.

She finally started eating better. Yesterday, she had half a shake and a bowl of chicken and rice from the restaurant across the street. That made me incredibly happy. I showed her a photo of her niece Lola today and her blood pressure shot way up. The nurses came running in. Lexi started crying. I made a note not to do that again. She gets upset easily, and I don't want to cause her more pain.

She wrote her name and "LEXI loves U" on a piece of paper. I sent that to her friends. Ray came to stay with her, allowing me to get some sleep. I wanted to go to bed and not get up for a month. Every day when I woke up, the first half a second, I would hope this was a bad dream; then reality would come crashing down.

Day 37: Saturday, June 24

She slept okay. According to the chart in her room she was up at one a.m. and six a.m., but when I arrived at seven a.m., the lights and TV were on, but she was asleep. It was great to have Ray here; he was my rock. It was much easier to have someone else. I could go to the store or do laundry without being in such a rush. We hated leaving her alone.

When the doctors came in today, they told us that Lexi is the star of the floor as they are very pleased with her progress. I'm so proud!

The eye doctor came in and said he could see damage to her optic nerve when he looked in her eyes, which is why her left eye wasn't opening. It may improve with time, but there was no way to know.

Last night there was a fashion show. It is one of Shepherd Center's major fundraisers and they invite previous patients to be models. The nurses and I were talking about it and they had asked me if Lexi would come back next year to participate. I said yes. Lexi asked if the models had their makeup done and wore fancy clothes. They told her they did. She decided she wanted to have her makeup done. I am not sure if she was confused and thought she would be a model, but it didn't matter. I had brought her makeup with us to Atlanta and one of the nurses offered to do her face for her. Her aunt had sent her a shirt from a big department store that she loved and we put her in that. This was the first time at Shepherd Center that she had worn makeup and her hair was brushed out. She looked beautiful. I pushed her in a wheelchair to where the fashion show was. We couldn't stay as it was too much for her. It is hard for brain-injury patients to be in a space with lots of noise, crowds or bright lights. I was hoping this would eventually improve, but for now she couldn't handle it. I was disappointed because I had wanted to see the fashion show. She was so agitated that once we returned to her floor, I had to push her around to try to calm her down. When we went by the nurse's station, she told them, "I want to check out."

Ray's best friend's parents were in Atlanta visiting one of their sons and they came by Shepherd Center to see us. They brought flowers; unfortunately, I was at yoga. Lexi called Ray "Dad," and he cried. He stayed with her until 11 pm. He had to put the mitt on her because she was pulling off the trach bandage. He would put on the mitt and she would pull it off and laugh. He said he laughed his butt off.

I went to a peer support group that Shepherd Center offers. I didn't go to as many of those meetings as I would have liked because I hated to leave her. They had very good information and I highly recommend them. Some patients were worse off than Lexi, and some progressed much faster. You will hear that every brain injury is different and that is true. It depends where your brain is injured and how severely. It also depends what you started with, as well as your health and age. I remember they told us in the ICU that if she had been 40-years-old, she would have been "toast," but she had her age going for her. The volunteer who drove me to do some shopping when we arrived in Atlanta told me about her husband, who had two doctorate degrees and was incredibly intelligent. He had a stroke and had recovered well. She felt that people with a good intellect recovered better. Lexi was incredibly smart and hopefully that will help her in this battle. *I was holding on to that like a lifeline!*

A young man and his mother were at the support group. Hurt in high school, he was now attending college. They talked about getting special accommodation through the disability office of the college. He had one seizure. I am terrified of seizures. His mom tracks him on his iPhone. He uses lists to get through the day. The doctor told his mom that he has a lot of dead brain matter. That haunted me for a long time. The mom said she slept outside of his bedroom door after he came home from the hospital to make sure he was safe. The mom said she deals with grief years later, but she describes her son as more open and he enjoys life a lot more. That was hopeful. This meeting really helped me know how to plan for Lexi's return to school.

They told us that TBI patients don't know how to do simple things they could do before, such as addressing an envelope. Lexi didn't know how to read a clock, and didn't know where she was or what day it was. We told her every day where she was and why, as well as the day and the time. Part of that was her short-term memory loss.

This meeting helped me think about things I would need when we were back home. We had an alarm system, but I would need to add window contacts on the upstairs windows alerting me that she opened a window. I didn't want to sleep on the floor outside her door like the other mother did. Ray and I talked about moving her into the bedroom across the hall from us, but Ray was adamant that he wanted her in "her" bedroom. We would cross that bridge when she was home.

Day 38: Sunday, June 25

Lexi was asleep when I arrived right before seven a.m. She woke up when they came in to take her vitals. I took off the mitt and she immediately removed the trach bandage. She said the "aquarium" under her hurt. I finally figured out it was her monitoring box. She had wires attached to her that would constantly monitor her vitals. She was always pulling them off, which was annoying to her nurses, and us.

I took a photo of all the pills she was taking. For a person who doesn't like to even take something for a headache, she was on a lot of medications. They weighed her yesterday and she was down to 98 lbs. I called her doctor at home to see what her weight was before the crash and she was 120 lbs. She was literally skin and bones. She had been eating and I was hoping she had gained weight. Lexi was a picky eater before the crash and remains so. At Shepherd Center we would go to the main room to eat with all the other patients. The therapist recommended we sit in the corner with her back to everyone, thus she wouldn't get distracted. I knew she was coming out of it when she refused to eat eggs as well as any other hospital food.

We went to the garden today. The first two times I took her it was "too much." Ray and I took her yesterday and she did great. Today I saw a dragonfly. Ray said he saw lots of them yesterday when we were there. Last night I was out on the parking deck and when I asked Abby for "a sign," a dragonfly appeared. Lots of their friends were seeing dragonflies and in Native American lore dragonflies are a person's spirit.

Day 39: Monday, June 26

My notes:
God knows what day it is, maybe the 26th. She had a 102-degree fever last night and again this morning. They are doing a urine culture and blood work to figure out what is going on. Her left foot has been sore all weekend so they ordered another x-ray.

They continue having to drain her bladder; I wish she would pee; I beg her, push on her stomach, run water, anything I can do to help her pee. She hates when they drain it, it causes her a great deal of pain. It is anguish as a mother to see her in such pain.

She is shaking her leg a lot. They had to give

> her another picc line that is torture for both
> of us as they can't find veins. It would help if
> she had two good arms, but they can't use her
> left arm.
>
> The Children's' Hospital of Philadelphia
> describes a PICC line as, "A PICC line is a thin,
> soft, long catheter (tube) that is inserted into
> a vein in your child's arm, leg or neck. The tip
> of the catheter is positioned in a large vein that
> carries blood into the heart. The PICC line is
> used for long-term intravenous (IV) antibiotics,
> nutrition or medications, and for blood draws."

Lexi had a PICC line to give her the antibiotics through an IV, as well as any other medications she might need.

I visited with the family counselor. I talked about how I would feel going home, how hard it would be to leave, and the awkwardness people would feel around me. She said going home will help Lexi. She suggested I have a stock answer when anyone asks me how Lexi is, eliminating the need to go into details. She suggested, "Thanks for asking; she is slowly getting better; this is a long road." She told me my feelings would lessen in intensity. We talked about my grief for Abby and how we were going to tell Lexi. She explained that Lexi needed to have her short-term memory before we could tell her. We don't want to have to tell her more than once. She warned me that brain injury patients will often appear emotionally non-responsive when they learn of a death. She warned me to be prepared *for no response*. Unfortunately, Shepherd Center deals with this quite a bit.

A woman whose daughter was hit by a drunk driver four years earlier had reached out to me. When we spoke on the phone, she said her daughter had a difficult time in school. It was now two years after the accident and she had taken only one class. Her daughter remains in constant pain. The mother told me, "Don't ever give up." Her daughter works to educate the public about the dangers of drunk driving. I was impressed and inspired she was able to do something positive out of her experience.

The nurse asked Lexi what she wants them to call her, she said "Miss Taylor." Another sign of her personality shining through.

Day 40: Tuesday, June 27

Today was our one-month wedding anniversary. Lexi had another shower this morning. She needed another chest x-ray. I asked about the pain meds, and it was last given on the 25th, meaning her pain was okay on the over-the-counter products. Thank God for that.

> **My notes:**
> Her speech therapist is Alexis, who is beyond wonderful, not only in how she works with Lexi, but she helps us to help her. I wrote down what she told Lexi, so I could know what to do *I know things get confusing for you, it's okay. It's your brain filling in for you. Read things word by word. Your brain is getting stuck on a word; stop and take a breath and reset. You're doing everything right. When you get overwhelmed or in pain, take a deep breath.*
> The therapist added: When there is a lot going on, she will get tired and overwhelmed. She told me to sit back and don't react because it will overwhelm her. It is so hard for me to watch my brilliant 18-year-old daughter struggling to do what is a first-grade worksheet.

We took videos of many of the therapy sessions. Today she did squats and I filmed it and sent it to everyone. I filmed her walking and she looks much stronger and can walk farther every day.

Day 41: Wednesday, June 28

When I was leaving the apartment this morning, I saw reflected on a building what looked like a beautiful sunrise. I walked out onto the parking deck and took a few moments to breathe in the beauty. Lexi loved going to the beach to watch the sunrise when she was home. I cried and thanked God that she would have more sunrises.

Every day we would tell her what day it was, where she was and that she had been in an accident. The nurses or therapists would ask her later in the day the same questions. If she didn't know the answers, they would give her choices. Slowly she was able to often choose the correct answer. It was hard to watch my child not know the basics, even though we had told her a few minutes ago.

When I entered the room, the nurse told me Lexi had gone to the bathroom; I was happy. It is like when you have a baby. Yesterday she told me she needed to go to the bathroom, but no one was there to help her get to the toilet; I couldn't get her up on my own and she wasn't walking. I told her just to pee and it would be okay as she had on a diaper, and she did. Baby steps back to being herself.

The surgery to close her trach was scheduled for today. Marshall would be here with my car today. Now we would be able to get farther than we could walk, and once we go to "outpatient," we would need a car. Pathways, the outpatient facility that is run by the Shepherd Center, was located seven miles away, with no public transportation. Shepherd Center would train us how to safely get Lexi in and out of the car. Later we would figure out how to get the car home.

My notes:
Time is hard for her to remember—it is easier to remember things that change the least. Tell her, listen closely now as we are going to change subject. She is blowing through the goals they have set for her, making *huge* gains.

She continues to be super-emotional, and her speech therapist suggested we redirect her if there was no reason for her emotions. This will teach her mind what is correct and appropriate. All of this felt overwhelming. On that note, she cried when she saw Marshall. She also walked quite a bit without complaining.

Today she will have her third surgery, this one to close her trach hole. Her trach was removed in the original hospital, but it isn't healing correctly, and with this surgery she won't have a scar. The doctor will make the incision in a crease, and it won't be as visible. As much as I hate another surgery, I know down the road she will be grateful.

At 3:15 p.m., she was pushed to the hospital next door for surgery. Once we were there, it was about a three-hours' wait before they took her back to have the surgery. While we were waiting, I was trying to do some work and send some emails announcing my new position.

While she was in surgery, Marshall and I went to get dinner before he went back to the apartment. I was sitting by myself in a large waiting room when the doctor came out to tell me it went well. When he came up to me, I was crying because I felt all of this was very unfair. Tomorrow would be six weeks—and my life had been on hold. In some ways it seemed like 100 years, and other ways, like yesterday. I will fly home tomorrow for about two weeks.

Life does go on, bills need to be paid, etc. As gut-wrenching as it would be to leave, the counselor here said what I am doing at home will help Lexi. Plus, I wanted to sleep in my own bed and find some semblance of the new normal. I was very excited to start my dream job.

Day 42: Thursday, June 29

Yesterday, she had surgery to close her trach. She couldn't eat past midnight on Tuesday. The surgery was supposed to be at four p.m., but they didn't take her back to the operating room until 7:30 p.m., and didn't start the surgery until eight p.m. She was both hungry and thirsty. It was hard as I wanted to feed her, not only to make her more comfortable, but to put weight back on her. I was upset that it was this late. I was learning about "hospital time," always add at least four hours to any surgery time. It was that way in Virginia and now in Georgia. We finally returned to Shepherd Center at 10:30 p.m. One of the great things about Shepherd Center is they are right next door to a hospital, with a tunnel connecting the two buildings. If a patient needs surgery or a scan, they can be rolled to the hospital next door. The doctor was pleased with how the surgery went.

She spent the night in ICU where they could watch her after the surgery. I had warned them about her Houdini skills. Her eyes itched due to the anesthesia, causing her to scratch them. They had to put on a mitt and tie her down to the bed. This morning, the nurse told me how she moved her hand out and pulled the bandage off her neck. Luckily, she didn't hurt anything. He told me that she was the sweetest patient and he wanted to adopt her. Apparently, another nurse told her how pretty she was and she told the nurse she was pretty, too. They told me they could tell what a special relationship she and Marshall have. I have always been very proud of both of my kids, and how they love each other.

A few nurses who had been working when she first arrived couldn't believe how much Lexi had improved.

I would be leaving today, and that was torture. I hadn't been away from her since the crash. I was looking forward to going home and sleeping in my own bed with my husband, knowing she would be in Marshall's very capable hands. She would be moved back to her room later today. The surgeon told us no therapy until Monday, but we hoped they would do a little speech therapy with her. She can do that from bed. I don't want to waste a second of this golden time.

I left the hospital while she was in the ICU. It was very hard to leave. But once I was in the car and had driven away, it was like a huge weight had been lifted off my shoulders. I realized it was the first time in a long while I hadn't been running to get back to her. I hadn't realized how much of a burden I felt, and how much stress I was holding until I was in that car. It is hard for me to explain the feeling of release I experienced heading to the airport.

Working Effectively with Hospital Staff:

1. Be there for the doctor's early morning rounds. That is so important as it is the only time you will see the doctors. Ask the nurses what time the doctors do their rounds. Be prepared as it may be very early in the morning.

2. Take notes and keep in a binder or a notebook. This will help you keep track of everything the doctors tell you as it can be very overwhelming. It will also help you because if there are any questions, you refer back to your notes.

3. Ask the doctors lots of questions. Make sure you understand as much as you can and to the best of your ability.

4. The nurses have a tough job; they are taking care of both the patients and the families—and are an unbelievable resource. We had friends and family bring food to them all the time. It was a little token of how much we appreciated what they were doing for all of us.

5. Ask for a social worker or case worker. They can tell you what services are available, and guide you with what you should be doing, like filing for Medicaid or Social Security.

Chapter 10

Back to Some Sense of Normalcy

"Hopefully, this will be the hardest year of your life."
– Shepherd Center's family counselor

My life had frozen in place since May 19th, but now it needed to go on. It was weird being home. It was very, very hard for me to be home without Lexi. I cried all the time, especially if I went into her room. It was time to go to work. My new employer had been wonderful to hold my job for me. When I landed, I went straight to work before going home. My team lead had come in on her day off to show me around. It was nice to have some normalcy in my life. I had to go through their training classes, which were a ton of fun, with toys on the tables and dress-up items. It was like nothing I had done before. I felt guilty for missing so much work that I worked 10-hour days. I was beyond exhausted. I felt torn between wanting to be a good employee, and the guilt I had for not being with Lexi at the hospital. This feeling didn't go away while she was in Atlanta, and even once she was home. Any working mom knows the guilt we feel; that was multiplied.

Once back at work, as I was being introduced around, I could tell by the look on one of the manager's face that he connected me to the crash. This was to become my new normal. I remember talking to my son about how uncomfortable it was and he said it had happened to him as well. I didn't bring up the crash at work unless people asked me about it, and I never mentioned it to any of my customers. I put on my happy face and went to work. Lexi wanted to be normal, and I also wanted some normalcy.

This was a great job as it was a happy place for me. Both my boss and the general manager had told me they would work with me on my schedule. I was grateful. I was not an ideal new employee. While at work I would try to set aside my worries and meet new people and talk to my members and other guests. It is a big venue, and many times I was so overwhelmed I found a corner to cry in. For many, many weeks I would count how many weeks since the crash, so for a long time, Friday afternoons were tough. One Friday at the same time as the crash, I was sitting at my desk thinking about that with my head in my hands. My boss walked up and asked, "Are you okay?" I wanted to scream, *"Of course not, I will never be okay again!"* However, I said I was fine because I had to keep up the pretense.

While I was gone, on July 1st, Lexi went on her first outing with the Shepherd Center staff. They took the young patients to a pizza place; this was the first time she had been out. She ate an entire pizza, which was wonderful. I was happy anytime she ate as she was very thin. I remember when I told my friend who is a doctor how much Lexi weighed, she told me the weight would come back, but in the meantime, I wanted to constantly feed her.

On the 4th of July, Atlanta has a large run called the Peachtree Road Race. It is a big deal at Shepherd Center because it starts with a wheelchair race in which many of their former patients participate. There were signs all over town and the staff had told us about it. Marshall pushed Lexi down in her wheelchair to watch the race. We were worried she wouldn't be able to handle the crowds and noise, but she stayed the entire time, and even stood up for about a minute with the therapist holding a belt around her waist. A big milestone. She was given a whirly toy and a t-shirt. She loved it. Our goal is to go back so she can run the 5K part of the Peachtree Road Race.

One of her friends happened to be in Atlanta for a few days and wanted to see her. Because we lived far away, not many people could come visit her. Unfortunately, Lexi was having an extremely bad day when her friend was in town and I had to tell her she couldn't come to the hospital. Lexi was talking gibberish. I talked to her on the phone that day, and she didn't know "who the guy in the room" was. It was her brother! For her not to know Marshall upset me. That was the worst day she had at Shepherd Center. Of course, I was hundreds of miles away. I knew Marshall was taking great care of her and would fight for her like I would, but his devotion didn't make my heartache any easier.

While I was back home, Lexi started refusing to eat the hospital food, which was a good sign. Her refusal to eat eggs was a sure sign she was coming around. We had to bring in food from outside, and fortunately we now had a car. There were quite a few places close by and she loves chicken, and we had that all the time. The rest of us were tired of it, but she wasn't.

Initially any food brought in from the outside had to be approved by the speech therapist. I had Marshall ask if she could have a salad on July 5th and was told she wasn't ready for crunchy foods yet as she continued to learn how to eat and swallow. This was a long road.

Chapter 11

I'm Back in Atlanta

"There are two ways to live: you can live as if nothing is a miracle or you can live as if everything is a miracle."
– Albert Einstein

Day 49: Friday, July 7

I had been gone nine days, but it seemed like forever. One of the best things about being gone was I could see how much Lexi had progressed. It was hard to tell when I was with her 24/7. She asked me if graduation had happened. I told her yes, and that Marshall had received her diploma. She could now read the clock and she was moving a lot more than when I left. Every day the nurses would ask her questions, such as "What day it is?" "Where are you?" etc. In the beginning, they would give her choices to pick from. Sometimes she got them right, but more often she didn't. Now she was able to answer some of the questions. Although she wasn't sure what today's date was, she knew the 4th of July was three days ago. She asked me about the car crash. I avoided answering her and changed the subject. Her thinking was much slower and it was hard for her to remember things so it was easy to change the subject.

Lexi was fixated on having her phone. Like any other teenager, she lived on her phone. The police had it as evidence, so we couldn't give it to her if we had wanted to. We didn't want her to see what was on her phone, such as texts about the crash and learning about Abby's death. She cannot have access to social media. If she checked Facebook or Googled her name, she would have learned about Abby. Marshall came up with a plan to give her one of his old phones with a new number on it, and without a sim card, allowing her to text, but not get online. Being a new number, the old text messages wouldn't come through. We were able to control who had the number, so she wouldn't be bombarded with messages. She was fixated on getting her old phone back or at least getting her friends' numbers. On July 4th she had texted me to send her Abby's number—*and that broke my heart.* I was at work when she asked me, and when I called Steve Davis, we came up with a plan to tell her Abby had lost her phone. Some of the texts she sent me during that time were gibberish, such as "Do u Ghana ald lawsgup fgdb fed pizza." After a few days the staff told us to take her phone away from her; she needed to focus on therapy and rest.

Lexi said to me: "I want to go to college," and "I want to be a doctor." She knew she was supposed to be going to Hokie camp for all freshman at Virginia Tech. It is held at a 4-H camp at a lake off campus. It is a way to have fun with summer camp activities and meet the other freshmen, giving students a sense of belonging when their classes start.

She told me she needed a hand and that her balance was bad. They are giving her a new wheelchair that she could push with her feet to build endurance and muscles in her legs.

She was walking the entire length of the floor, and they were only holding her by the belt and not holding her hand. I took a video and sent it. Everyone was blown away. She was finally moving her left fingers, praise the Lord. When I saw that, I cried. The staples were removed from her arm yesterday. Marshall told me she was in a lot of pain getting them out. For some reason, she thought she was in the library at her high school when the staples were removed. On the positive side, she was much more responsive than when I left. She was also now standing and pivoting into her wheelchair instead of being lifted out of bed. Her walking was substantially improved, as well as her short-term memory.

Unfortunately, she lost even more weight and now was down to 95 pounds, even though she was eating well—two pieces of pizza and eating almost an entire 9-inch take-out sub for lunch and dinner. We were trying to get her to drink a protein-packed drink during her breaks and at night. She was not liking that anymore, so they were bringing her ice cream that has lots of calories and protein. We waited to see how long she would continue to eat that. Hopefully this week she would put on some weight. She was working extremely hard, and sometimes had up to two hours of therapy without a break. To get to outpatient status, she must be able to handle up to five hours of therapy.

Today in physical therapy she danced with an older man who was there recovering from a stroke. Her therapist held onto Lexi's belt, but she was dancing. It was beyond awesome. His wife and I were watching with tears rolling down our cheeks. She told me he had never danced before. I never would have guessed that. Both of us were amazed at how well they danced together. I took a video and sent it to everyone.

Day 51: Sunday, July 9

This morning when the nurse gave Lexi apple juice with her pills, Lexi told her she didn't like apple juice. The nurse said, "I gave it to you a week ago and you drank it." Lexi said, "I don't like apple juice." Before the crash she wouldn't touch apple juice just like the eggs—*this is another sign she is coming back to us.*

Last night, her friend Ashley and Kelly, her mom, visited on their way to Ashley's university. Lexi gave Ashley a huge hug. Lexi ate a large piece of brownie that Kelly brought. Kelly and I left Ashley and Lexi to visit and went out for a drink. It was great to get out and be normal, even if it was for only a short time. Kelly told me the Saturday we were married that someone from a rival school posted "RIP Lexi" on Instagram, and everyone freaked out. She said she received at least 100 calls or texts. She sent a text to Nichole who was staying with Lexi during our wedding ceremony to make sure Lexi was alive. I was glad I didn't know anything about it. I did look back on my phone and saw a text from one of Lexi's friends asking if Lexi was okay. This was my first indication of how much on social media was posted by people who knew nothing about what was going on. Part of that was because there was silence from me, but it made me angry that lies were posted.

Kelly and I spent about an hour away; I knew Lexi was in good hands because she was in Shepherd Center and with Ashley. When we returned to the hospital, Kelly and Ashley stayed a little while longer. After they left, I asked Lexi if she and Ashley had a nice visit. She said yes, and that not much was new in Virginia. She is always complaining about how boring our hometown was. She said, "Mom, no one has forgotten me." I was completely taken a back. I told her of course people hadn't forgotten her; why would she think that? She said, "Because I am not on social media." I couldn't believe that she would even think that. She is so much more than social media. She had no idea the love we were getting not only from our community but from all over.

That morning she told me she slept well. She also said her left leg hurt a lot, and she had been tied down to the bed. We had talked to the doctor and she wasn't supposed to be restrained any more. I confronted the nurse who said it was on the hospital orders. I needed to talk to the doctor about this because the orders should have been changed. I know the nurses were doing their job, but it made me angry sometimes when what they were doing was detrimental.

You must be an advocate. No one else cares about your loved one like you do.

When the occupational therapists measured the vision in Lexi's left eye, it was 20/70. This was not good. They told us her vision may improve with vision therapy and time, and it could take up to a year. Back to that *magical first year*. Ray was flying back down to Atlanta and I had been texting him about other things we needed from home. Lexi wanted a strapless bra, so I asked him to bring one from her dresser. I tried to explain where they were. He ended up bringing one of her strapless bathing suit tops, making us all laugh a lot.

Day 52: Monday, July 10

I was leaving to go back home today, but before I left, I talked to the doctor about Lexi's foot pain. She was going to put her on another medication to see if that helped. Many x-rays of her foot were done and nothing was broken. They thought the pain was due to the brain damage. Would this never end?

Every time I left her, I felt like my heart was being ripped from my body. It was so painful!

In addition to everything else, we were trying to figure out how to handle outpatient living arrangements and care when I was not there. Ray or one of Lexi's brothers, Marshall or Vern, would be with her more than I would. She would need to shower and get dressed and we don't think she would be ready to do it alone. As I had mentioned, she has always been modest, and despite everything she had been through, we respected her privacy. Ray had talked to the caseworker who gave us names of two companies who could come in and help her with dressing and bathing. Because she wasn't approved for Medicaid yet, we would need to pay for this. Even though we wouldn't need help for more than an hour, the companies had a minimum payment time of four hours. Ray was adamant about needing this help, but I hated the idea of spending the money.

After thinking about Lexi's pain and how to best help her during outpatient care, I was grateful for good news: her speech therapist, was very, very pleased today. Lexi was able to pay attention and only needed to be told twice to look to her left. She was given a daily schedule in a folder, telling her where she needed to be. Being able to follow a schedule isn't only an important lesson in life, but also for college. Our goal was to get Lexi to college—and everything was designed to help her achieve that goal.

I left that afternoon. Every time I had to leave, I would cry and cry because I was so torn. I always knew she was in great hands with Ray being there, but it was torture being gone. We still couldn't let Lexi have access to social media because we hadn't told her about Abby, and we did everything we could to protect her. I texted Ray while waiting at the airport saying, "Watch your iPhone and iPad; she's fast."

Ray had to learn how to do a French braid for Lexi's hair. That was the best way to keep it smooth and out of her face. Before the crash, I would do a French braid in her hair every night, which was one of the highlights of my day. Lexi's hair is long and beautiful and I love brushing and braiding it for her. Most nights, she would sleep with the braid, and in the morning, her hair was wavy and cute. Even though Ray has a daughter, he had never done a braid before. Thanks to YouTube, he learned how quite quickly, and did a great job. He sent me a photo of his first braid and it was surprisingly good.

Ray used his family medical leave time to be in Atlanta. Once we were in outpatient, he was able to work remotely. His company was wonderful to us. Marshall's company was also understanding during this trying time. He was able to use vacation to be in Atlanta. He was a CPA, so we were lucky this wasn't tax season. We were all blessed to work for such fantastic companies.

On July 11th we received good news: Lexi's multiple pelvic fractures had healed quite well. The doctor had to look twice at the x-rays for the fractures because they had aligned so well. Ray did a great job taking notes while he stayed with Lexi, noting everything she ate, and she was eating a lot. However, we had another reminder of how fragile Lexi could be: Ray was told that we needed to contact our local fire department and let them know when she returned home. In case there was a fire, they needed to be informed she might need help getting out.

Ray was dealing with Lexi being upset about her phone. He texted me that she wanted to make sure I yelled at Apple and she hoped they cried. When I would remind her that the police had her phone, she would tell me to go down there and get it. When I talked to the fatal crash investigator and told him she was mad at him, he laughed and told me that "he could take it."

I was trying to work, trying to find a place for us to live once the apartment access ended, and micromanaging poor Ray. I texted him and asked what Lexi was doing. He said she was sleeping; I responded to not let her sleep too long, so she could then sleep through the night. He texted me back: "Honey, I know what I am doing. She has and will be working hard. She is sleeping through the night."

On July 12th she was walking without assistance. It took her only a few days once they put her in a "walking" wheelchair to go from sitting to walking. She is very determined to get out of there.

As soon as we arrived in Atlanta, I began looking for housing. Shepherd Center had housing onsite, but it was only for the first 30 days the patient was staying in the hospital. You could get the housing back once you were in outpatient, but we would have a gap. The average stay inpatient at Shepherd Center was eight weeks, meaning that many families need to find housing for that window between inpatient and outpatient. I knew the director of Ronald McDonald House in Virginia because they were my clients. I called her to ask if she could make a phone call to help us get into the center in Atlanta. I asked her to pull any strings she could to get us in there. I had also gone through the housing list that Shepherd Center had provided us. There was a low-cost option on the grounds of a church, so now I was on that list, too. I had asked everyone I knew for any connections they had to get us housing. Shepherd Center is in Buckhead, an affluent part of Atlanta. I was hoping that we could find someone who had a guesthouse or extra room that we could use. The furnished apartments available for short-term rentals in the area ran about $3,000 a month.

My best lead for a short-term furnished rental in the area was $1,500 a month. We needed to be very close to Shepherd Center because we were at the hospital most of the time. Many people sent me leads, from my neighbor to friends and acquaintances. We wouldn't know about Ronald McDonald House until the last minute, because it all depended on whether they had a room available. The day before we were to move out of the apartment, Ronald McDonald House called to say they would have a room for us. Ironically, I also learned the home on the church grounds would be available. I told them thank you very much, but we didn't need it, and to contact to the next person on the list.

On July 12th, Ray moved out of the apartment and into Ronald McDonald House. That same day Ray's sister, Olga, was flying in from California to stay with Lexi for a week. Her flight was supposed to get in at 3:45 p.m., but it was delayed. She wasn't going to get in until about midnight, and no one could enter Ronald McDonald House after 11 p.m. While I was in a training class at work, I walked out of the training room and used my phone to find a hotel for Olga. I felt bad because the hotel I found close to the airport ended up being nasty place to stay.

The Ronald McDonald House was beautiful and much larger than the one in Virginia. It was about a 15-minute drive to Shepherd Center. Thank goodness we had my car. I stayed at Ronald McDonald House only one night, but Ray stayed longer because he was in Atlanta more than I was. He was blown away by the place. They had dinner every night for all the families. We normally were at the hospital until seven or eight. Every night they had dinner and put the leftovers in the fridge for the families that missed the serving time. They also had all kinds of cakes, cookies, and other snacks. Coke is based in Atlanta and is a major sponsor. They had a Coke machine that only cost 25 cents. Because I am a Diet Coke fanatic, both Ray and Marshall texted me about the machine. They did ask for a donation for every night we were there, which we gladly made.

The morning of July 13th Olga arrived at Shepherd and Lexi recognized her. Lexi had only met Olga once the previous Thanksgiving. Although Olga had been in Virginia after the crash for our wedding, Lexi remained in a coma until after Olga left. To have her remember Olga was a great sign.

Lexi has always been doggedly determined, and once

she gets fixed on something, she will drive you crazy until she gets it. The crash amplified her determination. As I have shared, Lexi loves coffee. She had been asking for it, and the doctor told her she could only have decaf. They explained that caffeine could lead to a seizure. Once you have one seizure, you are at a much greater risk for other seizures. If you have a seizure, then you can't drive for a year. Coffee became an issue because she wanted us to stop and get her favorite every day. We were getting her decaf, then it turned into a fight because she wanted regular coffee. Give her an inch, and she wants a mile. It was emotionally exhausting.

On July 13th, they tested her eyesight again. I wanted to know if it had improved. Ray texted that her distance vision was 20/40 and up close was 20/70, so it hadn't changed. I texted Ray back and said, "Well at least she has sight . . . everything is relative now. Hopefully it will improve." That night the restaurant where she had worked was having a fundraiser for her. Each summer they have a bartender contest to raise money for a local charity. I was very moved that they wanted it to benefit Lexi this year. I couldn't attend as I was working late. I didn't know if I could have gone without breaking down. They raised about twice the amount they thought they would. I was incredibly moved and appreciative.

Day 57: Friday, July 14

On Tuesday Ray was trained on how to get Lexi out of bed and he walked with her holding onto the belt and his hand. She walked quite far that day with Ray. On Wednesday she was walking without support. She was eating super well because we were getting her outside food. She was supposed to go out with recreation therapy to her favorite chicken place earlier in the week, but she was getting her IV at the time and couldn't go. The next week, she was scheduled to go to the mall as her outing, and her Aunt Jamie would be there. All I could think is: Watch out stores.

On July 15th Ray flew home and left Lexi in Olga's capable hands. That same day Summer returned to Atlanta to see Lexi. I have a fantastic photo of them with huge smiles.

I continued training for my new job. After the classes, as a manager you must shadow each position, so you understand what everyone does. I had never worked in the hospitality industry before, making everything new to me. I enjoyed the training. During the classes I was the oldest in the group as most people were in their teens and twenties. At one point another trainee asked me if I was a spy. I laughed and said no; everyone needs to go through the classes.

It was great to be home with Ray for a week and a half. We went to our friend's house for dinner, the first normal thing we had done in a while. We took our grandkids to a kids' gym and then all went to breakfast. Every little thing we took for granted before suddenly felt wonderful.

Lexi was working hard at therapy. On the 16th of July, Olga texted me that she was up at 8:15 a.m., had coffee for breakfast, walked for 40 minutes, did 10 squats and walked up the stairs from the first floor to the second. They had been playing Uno and a memory game. On July 19th Olga texted, saying, "Lexi is so smart. She described what a brain is made of". When Olga asked her how she knew that, she said she remembered it from high school. Olga said, "A doctor in the making for sure." I shared that story with her biology teacher.

Lexi wasn't showing any interest in reading any of her cards or letters. While Olga was there, a friend of mine from California sent Lexi a card that Olga read to her but luckily, she read it in advance because it expressed sorrow at Abby's death.

Day 62: Wednesday July 19

Notes I wrote while I was home:
It's two months after the crash, and in some ways, it seems like this nightmare started a 100 years ago. Time has no meaning; even now I work to get through each day. I am grateful she has come so far; 60 days ago, we didn't even know if she would live. I had seen a friend of the girls who had arrived at the hospital shortly after Marshall. Photos of the crash were on the news, and she was certain that Abby was dead. She told me her dad was in the room with Steve when he heard the news, and neither of them could sleep for days as they were haunted by Steve's scream when they told him Abby was gone. I remember my friend Nichole told me she saw Steve taken back to a private room, and she also heard him scream. She said she had never experienced anything like it; it was horrific!

I am going to have to deal with Abby's death, maybe this weekend. The trauma we have all suffered is beyond belief. When I was at the church meeting Lexi's friend and her mom, the pastor came in to talk to me. He said his daughter was on that road five minutes earlier. Why them? We should have been at college orientation on the day she finally walked on her own. We should be planning for college, not outpatient at a brain injury rehabilitation hospital.

She's doing very well. One of the doctors asked if she wanted to hurt herself or anyone else. Her reply: "Yes, the doctor who told me I couldn't have caffeine!" That's my girl! Her personality is coming back more and more every day. We have explained to her that she needs to be able to do therapy for five hours straight with no nap once she goes to outpatient. She said she can do that if she can have caffeine. We reminded her that caffeine may cause seizures, and she was not allowed caffeine for a year—*she was not happy about that.*

I don't know how she is going to deal with all the attention once she gets home. People don't know what to say to Marshall and me. What about her?

This is all a million times worse than anyone can imagine.

Day 63: Friday, July 21

Her Aunt Jamie flew in from California on July 19th to take over for Olga. I scheduled everyone, allowing for some overlap so the person who was leaving could update the person who would now be "on duty." I had a list of things for the caregivers to know that the doctors had recommended to us. Rotating people in and out was working well.

The weekly outing for adolescent patients gives them a chance to get out in society and do normal things they will do once they are out of the hospital. This week it was going to the mall. Going to the mall for a brain injury patient can be quite stressful. They're dealing with crowds, possibly loud sounds and an unfamiliar area. Unfortunately, Aunt Jamie couldn't go with her; it was only for patients. I know Ray gave her money; probably Olga and Aunt Jamie also gave her money. Aunt Jamie sent me a photo of her in her hospital bed wearing a Virginia Tech t-shirt, holding her favorite coffee, with her new purchases laid out in front of her. She told me she had a dollar and some change left over. I sent the photo to a bunch of her friends. They noticed her left eye was much more open than it had been before. Her smile was wonderful, she loves shopping. Much later she asked me why we let her go shopping when she was so out of it, she doesn't like anything she bought then. However, at the time she was very proud of herself.

I was also micromanaging Olga and Jamie all the time because it was hard not to be there. Jamie told me Lexi was getting her sass back. That Thursday Lexi had made butter beer fudge as part of the adolescence activities. As a Harry Potter fan, she thought that was great.

She was walking on her own and going up and down the stairs. We told her she needed to be able to walk the stairs before she came home, so she could get to her bedroom on the second floor. When we gave her a goal, she was blowing through it.

On the 21st, Jamie texted me that Lexi said, "Four more days till my mom comes." She wanted to know when we could talk. It turned out that Lexi's memory didn't come back until Olga was there, so she didn't remember Ray, Marshall or me being there. That is why she kept asking Aunt Jamie to call all of us. Jamie didn't tell me this until I arrived. It broke my heart to have her think that we hadn't been with her. I remember the staff had told us she wouldn't remember all the bad stuff, but I didn't think she wouldn't remember any of us being there. *I will never recover from that.*

She asked me today to get Abby Davis's number. Oh God!

Day 64: Saturday, July 22

I was home and finally going to yoga at the Y for the first time in 10 weeks. My class started at eight a.m. I went in the yoga room and rolled out my mat a few minutes before the class was to begin when I saw Jamie had called. I walked out of the room and called her back. Before Jamie arrived at Shepherd Center that morning, the nurses had taken Lexi into the bathroom and left her in there. Shepherd Center had told us not to leave her alone, but they did. She stood up and fell. Lexi told Jamie; the nurses didn't. I also didn't get a call; they had both my and Ray's cell numbers on the board in her room. My first question to Jamie was: "Did she hit her head?" Once you have a brain injury, if you hit your head again, you may not survive it. She had hurt only her foot. It was bruised and swelling. The nurses told Jamie they couldn't put ice on it until the doctor was there. It was Saturday so it took three hours for the doctor to arrive.

Both Jamie and I were furious. When I asked Jamie if she wanted me to fly down, she said not to, she could handle it. I called the woman in charge of her floor and left a scathing message. Finally, the orthopedic doctor came in and ordered an X-ray (great, another one). Her foot was broken so she would now have to wear a boot for four weeks. Luckily, it wasn't broken badly enough to require surgery. Lexi had started to walk on her own, and now we had this setback. We were all very upset. Aunt Jamie felt guilty, but it wasn't her fault. I felt Shepherd Center was a very special and unique place—and I continue to feel that way—but they never should have left Lexi alone. They didn't handle this incident well at all.

Being with Lexi was grueling, especially when you were by yourself. During the week, she had therapy, with built-in breaks so the patient could rest. Saturday was a short day for therapy, and Sundays were a rest day, and you were on your own during those times. The weekends were very hard if you were alone. Knowing this, I had asked people who had connections in Atlanta if they could find someone who could come sit with Lexi while Aunt

Jamie was there by herself to give her a break. Ray was there with Olga, so it was only this one weekend we didn't have backup. My friend Kelly had put me in touch with someone her pastor had recommended, named Gia. She was a professional nanny who came to see Lexi a few times. I offered to pay her, but she refused. She was a godsend. One of the families she worked for was a sponsor of the apartment floor at Shepherd. We took a photo of her and Lexi with the acknowledgement plaque in the apartment hallway so she could show the family.

Day 66: Monday, July 24

The hospital in Virginia called to tell me that Lexi's medical records had been compromised. Apparently when there is a "high-profile" case such as this, they do an audit. They found that multiple people had accessed her medical records. I was assured that everyone who took part was fired. Just another level of hell.

Day 67: Tuesday, July 25

Finally, Ray and I flew back to Atlanta. When we arrived, we held on tight to Lexi, telling her that we had been with her before even though she couldn't remember.

The crash made me realize how much we all take every little thing for granted. Lexi had to re-learn how to do everything. At last, she was able to take a shower using a bench. She was out of her wheelchair. She was also able to get herself dressed. They gave us suggestions to help her get more movement in her arm. They recommended routine chores such as hanging up her clothes, cleaning windows, sorting coins, and putting on her socks. I was happy to hear that I can tell her she needs to help us with chores as part of her therapy.

They measured her eyesight, and her left eye remained at 20/70. She was having severe pain in her left foot. I felt like this would never end. I wanted my healthy girl back.

I spoke to the neuropsychology doctor. Lexi's short-term memory had returned. She was able to remember what day it was and where she was. They felt it was time to tell her about the crash because she had been asking. She told me she thought Ray and I were in the car with her. I was upset me every time she asked about it. We agreed we would tell her about Abby tomorrow. How I had been dreading this. I called the Davises and told them. We had been warned that Lexi might be emotionally flat and not respond. It would be like ripping my heart out.

Day 68: Wednesday, July 26

My notes:
This is the day I have dreaded. At four p.m., we will tell her about Abby. I have not dealt with Abby's death and wanted to go to her gravesite before I came back to Atlanta, but I could not. Lexi is coming back to us; she is smiling. I am afraid of setting her back—afraid of what this will do to her. I can't imagine how hard this will be for her. I know what a hard time I am having dealing with the loss of her friend. I hope her other friends can help her. I will help her if she will let me, but she probably won't.

The occupational therapist told her yesterday that her arm isn't just broken but will never move. We talked about the possibility for surgery once the infection clears up. She said she will have surgery, but we don't know yet if that will be possible, and it will be another few weeks before we have an answer.

> The broken foot will set her back. She is defi-
> ant again, and that is the brain injury, but also
> part of her personality. I am very afraid she
> will get hurt again.

Lexi's dad, Keith, was in Atlanta. Ray and I had family training to learn how to take care of her once she is in outpatient and living with us. Keith was there to see her and to stay with her during the day while we had training.

At four p.m. the neuropsychology doctor came into her room. Lexi was in her wheelchair, and I was sitting next to her. Ray was on the other side of her, the doctor was across from her, and her dad was between the doctor and me. We started with the doctor asking what her last memory was before the crash. She said it was collecting money for the dance car. What she meant was the transportation bus for prom. The doctor explained to her that the crash happened when she was coming back from the beach and a drunk driver had overcorrected and hit them head on. The doctor told her Abby was driving. Lexi looked at me and said, "Is Abby okay?" We had agreed that I couldn't tell her, so the doctor said Abby was killed instantly. Lexi started to sob. The doctor said that how she felt was okay, and we would answer any questions. I put my arms around her in her wheelchair and we both sobbed. Ray put his arm around her. Lexi and I sobbed for a good hour. My head was behind her back, so she couldn't see me crying, but she felt it for sure. My heart was breaking into a million pieces for my daughter.

After an hour of crying, she joked that she needed a burger for sure now. We all laughed. Ray and I went to get the burger and she stayed with her dad. When we left to get the burger, she had her phone and was texting. I called the Davises and told them; *it was all damn hard.* After we returned with her burger, she ate and didn't mentioned

Abby. She talked to Summer on the phone and I heard her talking about Abby being gone. I stayed that night with her in case she woke up crying and needed me.

Day 69: Thursday July 27

> **My notes:**
> I spoke to the doctor about how to get through her feelings and her wanting to be normal. She suggested we acknowledge her feelings; acknowledge what she wants to do. Say, "I know this is frustrating." Turn the tables and ask her to think about why what she wants to do may be unsafe, help her reason through it. We need to provide concrete reasons, not only "because I said so." Be specific with what the impact could be. An example: "Your friends don't know how to help you walk." Provide safe alternatives and let her make the choice. She's lost control—give her some control.

We hadn't given her much access to her friends because we hadn't wanted her to find out about Abby before we were able to tell her. Now that she knew, she needed to grieve. Her friends were further along in the grieving process and hopefully they could help her. She was texting her friends this morning, but then we had to put her phone away because she was obsessing over it. One of the girls had told her about the t-shirts everyone had and asked if she wanted to see it. Lexi said, "No." The doctor would talk with her again today to try to get her to work through her feelings. We had family training to accomplish yet. Shepherd Center had an apartment on the floor that is the same floor plan as the apartments in the housing building. They offer this to families so they can practice living with the patient with support staff right outside the door. We had the apartment for two nights, the 27th and 28th. It was great to have her with us at night. The first night the nurse came in about two a.m. I was sound asleep, but woke up and saw someone with a flashlight walking around. I nearly had a heart attack because I thought Lexi was out of bed. She was extremely determined to walk, and I was afraid she would get out of bed and fall again. We talked to the nurse, and they gave us the belt to secure her to the bed along with a key for when we were in the apartment. This way when Lexi is asleep, or when we are not right there and she is in bed, she is locked in like she was in the hospital. She thought she was okay and wanted to get up on her own, but as we knew from the foot incident, she wasn't. She continued to wear the boot when she walked.

Yay! Ray and I were finally allowed to take her out of the hospital. We walked to her favorite coffee and chicken places. It was quite a long walk through Shepherd Center and under the tunnel to the street. The sidewalk was not even, and I was terrified. We had her support belt on, and Ray held her while I mostly held my breath and pointed out cracks and other hazards in the sidewalk. She was happy to be outside and we were happy to take her to her favorite places. I have a great photo of all of us with beaming smiles!

Day 70: Saturday, July 29

Marshall flew in today to help us. My friend, Dani, was coming to Atlanta for a funeral, so she came to the hospital and watched some of Lexi's therapy. I wanted to get something for the nurses, and Ray and I had decided on gift certificates for a manicure. We thought they would enjoy a little pampering. Dani and I went to get the certificates, and while we were there, we had pedicures. It was great to have some girl time and catch up with my friend.

A group of Lexi's friends sent her a package of ten goodies. It was so cute because each item had a note of encouragement on it. They sent her socks with cups of coffee on them and the note said, "Because no one loves coffee like you," and hair ties with a note that said, "Pull your hair back and kick butt in therapy." It was so great to see her laugh and love everything.

As part of getting ready to leave the hospital, Shepherd Center had to show us how to get Lexi in and out of the car. Although she was walking, she was wearing the boot, and we had another clog-type thing to put on her other foot to make both feet the same level. It was a pain for us to have to put the boot and clog on and off all the time, and it made it harder for her to walk. I was terrified that she would fall.

We had another outing planned. We were going next door to a restaurant for dinner. We would all be going: Ray, Marshall, Keith, Lexi, Dani, and me. Woo hoo, a party! Although the restaurant was next door, we took the car. It was quite a production getting Lexi into the car and buckled in. We went early so we were the only ones there. Our friends had given us a gift certificate to the restaurant after we found out we were going to Atlanta. I hadn't looked at it before, and they had written, "Congratulations on your marriage and getting Lexi into Shepherd." I was so moved I had tears rolling down my cheeks.

Day 74: Tuesday, August 1

Tomorrow, Lexi goes to outpatient—a huge, terrifying step. We would now be 100 percent responsible for her safety. So far, we had always had a medical professional to support us. This will be a new chapter and I am scared because it will now be *all on us*. It was hard to believe how far she had come.

Gia, our new Atlanta friend, came the night before to see us, and she noticed a huge difference in one week. I hoped Lexi would continue this spectacular growth. Today we received the results of her neuro psych testing:

- It was hard for her to remember twenty words; she has mild-to-moderate impairment.

- Did well (average) in verbal memory. We need to give her context. Help her to think like a story. Her verbal memory is a big deal. Her reasoning is reduced.

- Her higher-order cognitive function is bad, but we should see rapid gains. We need to give her clear instructions—when and where to use strategies, i.e. where things need to go.

- Her visual memory is good.

- Her processing speed is slow; give her time to process.

The doctor explained that after a brain injury, it's hard for patients to see their difficulties. It will be more noticeable when she leaves Shepherd Center. Transitioning home will be difficult because of the changes she has experienced.

Communication will be important between all of us. Each transition will be difficult due to adjustment issues.

Shepherd Center recommends that one-year post injury, a full, all-day evaluation be done with a neuro psych test. This will be needed for her to get accommodations in college. We asked about college and the doctor recommended she start with one on-line class. In the fall, she may be able to take a class or two. They recommended she take small steps. We need to make sure we contact the vocational counselor at school to get accommodations, like extra time for tests, getting notes ahead of time, etc. They suggested we keep multitasking to a minimum.

Today we were able to move back into the apartment at Shepherd Center from Ronald McDonald house. This time, between us, Marshall and I were able to clean the apartment right away. We had the apartment until we returned home. Hallelujah! I had spent so much time and energy worrying about our living arrangements that I was happy to put that behind me.

I had to go to the pharmacy at Shepherd Center to get her vast assortment of prescription drugs before we left inpatient. They had wooden signs in the window: the sign I thought summed up this journey the best: *You Never Know How Strong You Are Until Being Strong Is the Only Choice You Have.* I bought one for me and one for Abby's mom.

Ray had returned home to work, but Marshall and I were there for the last day of inpatient. They had a "graduation ceremony" with all of Lexi's therapists. She received hugs from many of her nurses. Before we left, we weighed her and learned she was up to 104 pounds so she was going in the right direction. Our goal had been for Lexi to walk out of Shepherd Center. I was told that very few patients were able do that. It was *amazing* when Lexi walked out under her own power. I cried to think about how far she had come. When we arrived seven weeks earlier, Lexi was in ICU for two nights. She could barely swallow; she couldn't walk; she couldn't go the bathroom; she couldn't feed herself; she was very agitated, biting and hitting and had to be restrained. She is the Shepherd Center's miracle we had heard much about. I had never been prouder of her and her hard-charging personality. She was a fighter.

To celebrate her release, first the three of us went out to lunch, and then she and I had a manicure and pedicure. During the manicure she wore her arm sling, and they worked around her fused arm, but it was awkward. I paid extra to have neck and shoulder massages; we both needed it. That night in the apartment I grilled vegan burgers and fresh corn. It felt so great to be able to make dinner and all be under one roof. Although it wasn't home, it was much better than a hospital room.

We put together a list of things she needed to do each morning before we left and then another list of things she needed to do before bed. This helped her feel more independent and we didn't feel like we were constantly reminding her. It was also useful considering that several people were coming to Atlanta to stay with her.

Take Care of Yourself

Yes, everyone says this—and it is true. It is very hard, and I didn't do a great job myself, but trying to do little things will help:

1. Get exercise when you can. I took the stairs instead of the elevator. Even when we had a car, I walked to the coffee shop or to get lunch.

2. Try to do at least one thing that brings you some joy. There are all kinds of apps that have positive thoughts that can be sent to you automatically each day. Look up a joke so you can at least smile, if not laugh.

3. I have done yoga for years and I found a yoga studio that I could walk to in Atlanta. I only went when someone else was in town, because I didn't want to leave Lexi alone. It was a great outlet for me. Once Lexi was in outpatient care, I took her to a class, too.

4. One of the best things about Atlanta was finding a massage therapist. I saw him a few times and he also worked on Lexi, especially her shoulder. He was a lifesaver for me.

5. Make sure you're eating healthy and try to get as much sleep as you can. As I have said, this is a marathon and you need lots of energy.

6. Ask for help. Ask for what you need; it may be cleaning your house, running errands, going to the grocery store or bringing you a meal or a cup of coffee. It will make the person who helps you feel better, too!

7. Find a support group because no one can understand like someone has been through a similar trauma.

Chapter 12

Lexi's Now Our Total Responsibility: August 3, 2017

"Where there is great love, there are always miracles."
– Willa Cather

Day 76: Thursday, August 3

Today we began the next step in our journey. Outpatient at Shepherd Center was called Pathways. It was going well. I really liked her team. There were other families we had met in the hospital. A young man's mom came up and hugged both of us and was delighted and couldn't believe how well Lexi looked. They had left for outpatient right after we arrived at Shepherds. It is breathtaking to see patients we had seen in the hospital and what they were accomplishing now.

There was a group of young people at Pathways, some of whom we hadn't met during inpatient. I have a photo of four kids all about the same age. I call it *my photo of tragedy*. There is Lexi who was hit by a drunk and drugged driver; a young man who was hurt on a motorcycle; a young woman who was bullied and assaulted; and a young woman who had been texting and driving and hit a tree. All of them were struggling with a traumatic brain injury. It broke my heart to see these promising young people. Life isn't fair. *It makes me aware a traumatic brain injury can happen in an instant to anyone.*

Lexi was continuing to complain about not being able to have caffeine in her coffee. She had a one-track mind, and it was way worse than it was before the crash. She couldn't be reasoned with. Pathways told her she needed to eat super healthy, because the food she eats is like a drug for her brain. I don't know why I didn't think about that. I was focused about putting weight on her and was giving her milk shakes, hamburgers, etc., not much that was good for her brain. We were now focused on eating super healthy.

Day 77: Friday, August 4

Doctors told us that TBI patients have a one-in-five risk of depression, which is higher than "normal." Alcohol and drug use will add to risk of seizures. We'll have no warning of a seizure, and if she has one seizure, she is likely to have more.

I have always been terrified of my kids having seizures. When Marshall was a few months old he was sick and running a fever and I woke him up in the middle of the night to check his temperature. I called the pediatrician when he had a fever to ask what to do. When I talked to the doctor, he told me, "Never wake a sleeping baby." Well, after that message, I didn't do that again, but my fear of seizures never went away. Now my girl was at a high risk of seizures because of this brain injury.

The therapists at Shepherd Center had suggested numerous card games and other things we could do to help her brain heal. We spent a lot of time playing those games in the apartment.

Day 81: Tuesday, August 8

One of the great things about outpatient is we can go out and do whatever we want with Lexi. On this day, I was back home trying to work and Lexi talked Ray into taking her shopping. They went to lunch and her favorite shops, and of course, she had her favorite coffee. He sent me a photo with her wearing her Virginia Tech shirt, laden down with her packages and coffee in her hand. I forwarded it to her friends. One of them responded back that it was about this time of the summer when Lexi would send a group message to them for a dinner at their favorite restaurant.

Day 82: Wednesday, August 9

All the work and arguing we did about someone coming in and helping her shower and get dressed was for naught; the nursing people never showed up. Ray was really upset. We let Shepherd Center know so they wouldn't recommend that firm again.

While I was home, I went to DMV to get my driver's license changed with my new name. I also had to suspend Lexi's driver's license. I remember when she passed her license test, only a few days after she was eligible. I was terrified of her driving, so I wanted to put it off as long as I could, but she would have none of that. I told her if she didn't pass the test, she would have to wait 30 days. She passed. We had talked to the security guard when we came in and told him she was there to get her license. He came up to her afterwards and asked if she passed. She said she did. He said it was unusual for people to pass the first try. She was so happy to have her license. She would be very upset that I was suspending it.

We had our meeting with the doctor from outpatient today. Lexi will be released and able to come home on September 21, four months and two days after the crash. While she is there the therapy will be five days a week for five hours a day. She will continue therapy once she is home. It was great to have a date when we would all be together again, and this insane traveling would end. I was *so sick of airports.*

Day 91: Friday, August 18

I had come home on the 6th and wouldn't go back until the 28th. That is a really long time. I was trying to stay focused on work as much as I could. I would go to work and then come home and sleep. Lexi and Ray had figured out a creative and safe way to do her showers and for her to get dressed. He would roll her into the bathroom and start the shower and lock her wheelchair in place, then leave while she showered. He would stand right outside the bathroom. When she was done, she sat down in the wheelchair and dried herself off. Because of her arm, she couldn't easily put on a bra, but they put a sheet over her while she sat on her bed and Ray helped her get dressed. He had pillows all around her, on kitchen chairs next to her bed; the night-stand next to the bed was piled with pillows and blankets so if she fell, she would land in a cocoon of softness. He sent me a photo of this "safety cocoon." I was scared she would fall, and I freaked out while she was showering and kept bugging Ray. He told me they had it. She was listening to him; it was a good thing I wasn't there.

She sat in her wheelchair when she put on her makeup. She had a beauty blender, which needed to be wet to use with foundation. She would call, "Oh, Ray" and he would wet it. She had taught him how to wet it and partially dry it, so it was just right. He played cards with her and did her vision therapy every night. He was now a master French braider.

Ray taught Lexi how to play pool and she wasn't bad. They passed the extra time by playing games and watching all the Harry Potter movies again and again and again.

Lexi had all her piercings removed in the emergency room and now wanted to get them back. She saw the infectious disease doctor today who told her no belly button or nose piercing. Of course, she agreed when the doctor was in the room, but afterwards she gave Ray grief. This was the pattern we will have to live with.

I am part of a Facebook page for Virginia Tech parents. The love and support we received from the Virginia Tech community was unbelievable. Nonetheless, it was hard to see the posts about others getting ready to start college. Many parents were venting about what I considered to be minor issues. It was a closed group, so I was able to post a few updates.

This was my post on the 18th:
As you get ready to take your children to school and worry about what you have left at home or have trouble lofting their bed, take a moment to be thankful you are there. Thirteen Fridays ago, our world was shattered by a drunk and drugged driver—who, in the middle of a sunny Friday, hit two beautiful girls who were excited about starting at Virginia Tech this month. Now instead of packing my daughter for school I am planning her fourth surgery and figuring out how we are going to stay an extra month in Georgia, as well as talking to our attorney and Social Security—and that is only the tip of the iceberg. And I'm the "lucky" one. Abby Davis was killed, a beautiful light snuffed out.

> At least Lexi is alive and improving, but her life will be forever changed. Thanks for all the love from this site and best wishes to the class of 2021. Lexi and Abby both wish they were there with you.

Day 93: Sunday, August 20

Yesterday it was three months. I wake up every day and think to myself this is so hard. I am barely functioning. It is a miracle I have kept my job. I am trying so hard, but I am overwhelmed.

Day 94: Monday, August 21

Ray remained in Atlanta as the primary caregiver. We flew her sister Ellie and her kids, and her brother Vern to Atlanta. Vern would stay a week and be the caregiver while Ray came home to work. We felt it was important for Lexi to see her sister, niece, and nephew. A few weeks ago, when I showed Lexi the photo of her niece, her blood pressure shot up and she started to cry.

Lexi's two-year-old nephew recognized her right away and literally held her hand the entire weekend. They all went to the aquarium. Lexi loves aquariums, and they all had a great time there. Ray flew home with Ellie and the kids; he said that was exhausting. It was great to be home with Ray for a little while.

Lexi had always been a handful as a teenage girl, but the brain injury made even simple things extra tough. We had been warned that brain injury patients might exit cars at a stoplight or while driving. In many ways she is like a young child in an adult body—and with the will of a teenager. We tried to have Lexi sit in the back seat, but she said it made her sick. She did get carsick before the crash, giving her a legitimate reason. Once we determined she needed to sit up front, we tried to tape the door handle, but she pulled off the tape. One morning we agreed to take her to the coffee shop, but then she was having a fit, so we drove away. While we were stopped, she tried to get out of the car. I grabbed her by the neck of her shirt to hold her back. It was terrifying for both Vern and me. They warned us about her behavior, but at times, I didn't know if I can do this.

I flew Lexi's good friend Emma down for a few days before she started college. I thought it would help her to have someone to talk to about Abby. I was back at home, so I kept asking for photos of the two of them together. The smiling faces in the photos made my heart happy. They should be a "priceless" commercial. They talked about Abby and Emma told her it was okay to be sad, and that she was sad, too. I had Emma go to the counselor with Lexi. Lexi wasn't opening up to the counselor, and I was worried about that. I also wanted Emma to hear what the counselor was telling her, so Lexi wouldn't say I was making things up.

Day 95: Tuesday, August 22

We should have been heading to Virginia Tech today for Lexi to start school. Instead she was in outpatient trying to recover and I was hundreds of miles away. She told Emma she should be at Tech about now, *so she is remembering.* Before Emma left, she texted me they were talking about Abby and laughing and smiling—that made me feel happy. I know that is what Abby would have wanted. Emma will leave tomorrow, but it had been good for both of them to see each other. Emma said she is the same Lexi. Emma's mom had texted me that Emma was very happy to see Lexi.

Outpatient was like middle school. While we were

in-patient, we were encouraged to go to therapy with her; however, now that we were in outpatient, they didn't want us to observe it. Part of it was they didn't have enough room for the families in the therapy room. Ray and the other parents spent time in the kitchen doing work.

During outpatient they did a treatment called needling. They put needles in Lexi's left shoulder to loosen the muscles that hadn't been used in such a long time that they had frozen up. The needles really hurt but she could move her shoulder better. Her range of motion was getting better every day.

Day 96: Wednesday, August 23

We started vision therapy. The doctor did a vision exam and Lexi needed both reading and distance glasses. He put a prism lens on her glasses to see if it helped to compensate for her vision loss. Before the crash she needed distance glasses and we had them in Atlanta, so we were able to reuse the frames. For a second set of glasses, she chose a very expensive pair, and in my absence, Ray let her get them.

She went to see the orthopedist who said he could do surgery on her left arm, giving her some movement in it. However, he couldn't do it until right before we are scheduled to come home. He would need to see her at least weekly after the surgery. That would mean another month in Atlanta with no housing. I was looking for doctors near home who could do the very complex, rare surgery.

Day 97: Thursday, August 24

I was back in Atlanta again. Ray and I got to spend the weekend together. I was tired of all the flights. It was costing us a fortune and being summer, there were no deals.

I felt blessed to be working for such a great company and with wonderful people who gave me a flexible schedule. I was trying to be a great employee, but it was hard.

Day 99: Saturday, August 26

Two of Lexi's friends were going to be in Atlanta on their way to college; I invited them for a sleepover. We took the girls to dinner and Ray and I sat in another room of the restaurant. We told them they would have to pay if they didn't sit with us, but Ray surprised them by picking up the tab. He did check to make sure Lexi didn't order root beer that's full of caffeine. It was good to know she made a good choice with her beverage. That night there were five of us in a small room with one bathroom for a sleepover. It was close quarters, but we made it work. I asked the girls to make sure they went to sleep early because Lexi needed her sleep.

Her friend sent me the Instagram posts from Abby the day of the crash. There is one of Lexi catching something, which is the last photo I have seen of her with her left arm straight.

I found a doctor at the University of Virginia who thought he could do the surgery. I scheduled an appointment after sending her records and talking to his assistant. We had an appointment to see him right after she gets home.

The next chapter would begin soon, and I was sure it would be full of challenges.

Day 107: Saturday, September 2

My notes:
I can't believe it's September; this has been the lost summer. I am back home by myself.

Yesterday, Lexi texted me asking which tattoo she should get to remember Abby. I couldn't respond as no one should have to make that choice, let alone an 18-year-old. I broke down in tears. Luckily my work is a large place because I often must go find a quiet spot to break down and cry.

Day 114: Saturday, September 9

My notes:
Happy, happy, joy, joy. I left early this morning to head back to Atlanta. It is always good to be back and see all the progress she has made. She finally has the boot off and is walking much better. Breaking her foot was a real setback. This is the last time I will be in Atlanta before she comes home. I am here for family training for what we need to know before she comes home. I must get the apartment ready to move out. My friend, Kelly, whose daughter is going to college in the south will drive my car home. That is great because we don't need to make the drive, and Kelly gets a free flight to Atlanta and saves a ton of time. I need to get the car packed up as much as possible, so Ray won't have that much to do because he has Lexi to take care of.

I flew her friend, Summer in for a few days. While Ray was in town, all four of us went to an Atlanta Braves game. Ray had bought the girls matching Braves hats and t-shirts. Because TBI patients are often upset by crowds and noise, I was worried that the game would be too much for Lexi, so I bought cheap seats thinking we would only be there for a short time. Ray is a huge baseball fan and had never sat that far up. It turns out we could see the entire field, and he liked it. We all had a lot of fun. Lexi handled the noise and crowd fine, reaching an enormous milestone.

As if not enough had happened that summer, a hurricane was heading toward Atlanta. Ray flew home before the storm, so I was with both girls. We had stocked up on food and water and had games to play and movies to watch. It ended up being just a lot of rain, but we lost a day of therapy due to power being out at Pathways.

We had a great time with Summer. After being confined to a hospital room for months, it was so great to get out. I took the girls to explore Olympic Park in downtown Atlanta, where we went on a big Ferris wheel. After being cooped up for a few days due to the storm, we were all going stir crazy.

Here are my notes from the family training:

- *Safety*: She will need someone with her. We need to be careful around crowds, be on extra alert for others around her. She may be mentally fatigued from being around others.

- They told us to keep playing games with her and have her do apps like Lumosity and Shockwave.

- *Physical therapy*: Said her balance is good, but her left foot was not as good as her right. She can skip and hop. Her left shoulder isn't moving as much as it should. It didn't move for a long time, they have been working on it. They are going to put in dry needles today to loosen up her muscles.

- She continues to need help problem solving. Have her help us when we go to the store; ask, "Where is the cereal?" "What do you put on cereal?"

- *Occupational Therapy*: She needs to work on turning her head and scanning side to side when she is walking. We need to talk an orthopedist about her arm. She may need hand therapy and that is specialized, thus we need to check on it. We need to have her do things to help her arm move, like mopping, sweeping, reaching to put away dishes, etc.

Day 123: Monday, September 18

I flew back home yesterday for the last time. I am so glad all this travel is almost over.

My notes:
On Thursday, September 14, Lexi had water therapy, and she had her swimsuit and towel in her school backpack. We were in Atlanta, driving back to the apartment when she asked for lip cream. I told her she had some in her backpack. When she was looking for it, she said, "Whose keys are these? They aren't mine." I glanced down and saw the Tech lanyard. She said again they weren't hers. I told her no, because hers were at home hanging on the peg where she kept them. When we parked, I looked down and saw the Honda key and knew they must be Abby's. No one had asked me about missing keys, and Abby wasn't alive to

ask. I took a photo and texted the Davises, and yes, they were Abby's. Terri had been asking the police for them. Apparently, Abby had lost them two days before the crash in the lunchroom at school. One of the last texts the Davises received was, "OMG Lexi has my keys!" Apparently, Lexi had told Abby that she had found her keys, but they were in her school backpack that was at home.

I was leaving Atlanta for the last time three days later. I put the keys in my carry-on, so they wouldn't get lost. I had a long necklace with an angel wing on it that I was going to wear home, but it didn't look good with my shirt, so I threw it in my carry-on in a separate area from the keys. When I returned to Virginia, the necklace and keys were tangled together, and I couldn't untangle them. I figured that Abby was sending me a sign that she wanted her mom to have this necklace. I went to the Davises the Monday after I returned home and gave them the keys and explained the necklace. Abby's brother had held the keys while we were talking and tried to pull the necklace off, but it didn't budge. He gave the keys back to his mom and she was holding the keys in her hand, not messing with them at all, when the necklace simply fell to the floor. We all looked at each other with wide eyes and got chills. It was a sign from Abby for sure.

Day 124: Tuesday, September 19 – Four months since the crash

We had a conference with the doctor about coming home. Lexi and Ray were with the doctor in Atlanta, and I was on the phone.

Here are my notes:

- She is doing better on the attention drug they prescribed. Her appetite is good and the vision will take time. Her nerve pain in her foot is getting better so we are cutting back the nerve damage drug to one pill at bedtime for a week, and then try to stop it completely. Her elbow is hurting a lot, especially when you touch it. Give her Tylenol; no Aleve or Motrin.

- We talked about her insistence on a subject like coffee. They said part of it is her age; we are to try to re-direct her or drop it as it will escalate. Home won't be the same; she is not the same Lexi as before the crash. There will be restrictions for now, like things it is not safe for her to do.

- *Speech*: She is not consistent. Her impulsiveness is working against her. Her higher-level executive functions are not working, meaning she cannot make major decisions. She must plan everything and double-check things. We need to make her accountable for doing things around the house; if she misses something, show her. This will build awareness. Self-awareness is a higher-level function. Her brain is working in a new way. (Read more about executive function on page 174.)

- Schedule is important. A schedule will help her memory and attention and help her to predict what is happening next. She needs structure and routine. She needs to be responsible. We need to let her figure things out on her own, and loosen the leash a little bit (that comment was to me, I know.) Failure will help her brain learn more than success.

- Therapy is recommended two to three times a week once we are home. They are sending the reports to the local hospital where she will start therapy, so the therapists will know what she needs help with.

- We need to be her advocates.

- Look at auditing a college class in the fall.

- On the rating scale for supervision, the highest is a ten. Lexi is an eight; this means we need to check on her every thirty minutes.

- We expressed our concern because she is driven to go to college, and she insists she doesn't want to be behind her class. The doctor explained college will be there; it's not like high school where people know what year you are in. She needs to go at her own pace and can't be compared with anyone else. Stress can be overwhelming for her and is bad for her health. It can lead to depression. Go at your own pace. Take it step by step.

Executive Function

Headway.org.uk, a TBI website based in the United Kingdom, describes it as follows:

> Executive functioning is an umbrella term for many abilities including:
>
> - Planning and organization
> - Flexible thinking
> - Monitoring performance
> - Multi-tasking
> - Solving unusual problems
> - Self-awareness
> - Learning rules
> - Social behavior
> - Making decisions
> - Motivation
> - Initiating appropriate behavior
> - Inhibiting inappropriate behavior
> - Controlling emotions
> - Concentrating and taking in information

Most of us take these abilities for granted and we effortlessly perform extremely complex tasks all the time in our everyday lives. Let us consider, for example, the role of some executive functions in a "simple" activity like cooking a meal:

- Motivation–Wanting to make a nice meal and making the decision to start doing it.

- Planning and organization–Getting all the ingredients and thinking about the right times to start them cooking so they will be ready at the same time.

- Monitoring performance–Checking that the food is cooking properly and the water isn't boiling over.

- Flexible thinking–Lowering the heat if the food is cooking too quickly or leaving it longer if it is not cooked.

- Multi-tasking–Washing the laundry and putting it out to dry, while also remembering to attend to the food at the right times.

Day 127: Friday, September 21 – Homecoming Day

I wrote in my journal: Today is the day, so excited but scared. Such an emotional week.

Ray was with her the last week in Atlanta. The final day they were at Pathways in the morning for therapy, then she graduated. When someone leaves Pathways, there is a ceremony with a large graduation hat. It was not the graduation we had planned on, but it was very sweet. I was in Atlanta for her graduation from Shepherd Center and Ray was with her for graduation from Pathways. She was excited to come home. Normally they have people spend the entire day in therapy, but she didn't want to, so we negotiated that she could be there a half-day and then leave, allowing them to make the flight. Ray had gone back to the apartment to finish cleaning and checking out while she was in therapy. He was back in time to take lots of photos of graduation. Then it was back to Shepherd Center to drop off the car and get to the airport. She walked through the Atlanta airport, which is very large. This was something we couldn't even have imagined when she first arrived in Atlanta.

She wanted to fly home first class. We had spent so much money on travel so I decided what the heck, and she and Ray flew home together first class from Atlanta.

My employer had an event to promote their holiday parties. I had invited my members, so I was there until I had to leave to go to the airport. It was good for me to stay busy that day. Six of her close friends were at the airport along with all the family. It was wonderful to see her walking off the airplane. I fought back tears as I think everyone did. Ray had bought her a coming-home dress and she looked beautiful. I couldn't help but think about how we had left Virginia with her being on a stretcher, agitated, biting, and hitting.

Her friends had a sign welcoming her home and they all gave her big hugs. It was the first time most of them had seen her since the crash, and for the few that had seen her, it was when she was right out of the ICU in the hospital. She was much, much better now. She looked like the old Lexi even though she wasn't.

That is the problem with a brain injury—it is the hidden injury. Often TBI victims will look fine. However, your brain is what makes you who you are; it controls your emotions, temperature, thinking, everything. She had come very far, but had a long way to go.

I allowed her friends to come over to the house after the airport, but I didn't let them stay long. It was a long and emotional day for us all.

How to Handle Always Having Someone There Once You Get Home:

1. Try to plan your schedule in advance so you have coverage when you can't be there. I occasionally needed someone last minute, which was much harder—so plan ahead as much as you can.

2. When asking for help, be as specific as possible so helpers know what to expect. Everyone wants to help, but not everyone will actually come through. NOTE: You probably know who will actually come through for you. When Lexi was about to come home, I emailed the people who had offered to help, explaining what I would need—specifically. I asked them to respond if they were still willing to help, and to include what times and dates they were available. I also asked for the best way to reach them. Some people were only available in the evenings or on certain days, but that was fine. I carried that contact list with me so if something came up, I could go down the list and ask for help.

3. Try to give yourself a break. Have a trusted family member or friend come over so you can get out of the house. My son was wonderful; he would take Lexi out to eat or just to hang out with her at his house. It gave us a break and allowed him and his sister to spend time together. As the adult, try to use that time to re-connect with your spouse or partner or take time for yourself.

4. If you use an caregiver agency, they will find some-one to cover if the caregiver can't come for a day or calls in sick. It didn't happen often, but when it did that was a big help. If it's a family member or friend, make sure you have a backup plan.

Chapter 13

Preparing for Home

"Diamonds may be precious, but daughters are priceless."
– Unknown

Before Lexi came home, I had to get the house ready. We were blessed to have many people offer to help us make changes to the house. Luckily, we only needed minor improvements. In the beginning, I had talked to a mom whose son suffered a TBI and was in a wheelchair. We had looked briefly at options if that was the case. Then we were told that most TBI patients could walk. Often there will be other medical issues requiring a wheelchair. We were past the wheelchair stage by the time she came home.

She needed to be able to go up and down stairs in our two-story home. When she met that goal before she left inpatient, it was one of the scariest times in the hospital for me. I was afraid she would fall down the stairs in the beginning. Her therapists knew what they were doing, but it did terrify me.

Because her arm couldn't straighten, I wanted a hand railing on both sides of the stairs. I found a volunteer to install a second railing.

Her bathroom had a tub/shower combination and I was worried about her being able to get in and out of it safely. Her physical therapist suggested we have a walk-in shower installed. We had wonderful volunteers that put in a new shower that was easier for her to use.

In addition to getting the house ready, I had to find doctors and set up physical, occupational, speech, and vision therapy. I had interviewed three different therapy places before she came home. I had seen a story on Shepherd Center's Facebook page about a local family who had been there. The man was in a motorcycle accident and was badly injured, but was now working, and he and his wife had a new baby. I had posted on Facebook that I needed to find them, and about 10 minutes later, someone sent me a message with the woman's Facebook page. She was a great resource. She was able to tell me about her husband's therapy and other resources they used when he was home. They had tried various speech therapists and found one they loved. I tried to find her, but she wasn't working at the same center. I learned she was going back into practice at the hospital about 15 minutes from our house. Because of that, I chose to do Lexi's therapy at the local hospital even though I had looked at other local places.

Because we were told not to leave her home alone, I needed to find a "caregiver" for her to allow us to go to work. This was another place I used my resources and asked for help. I had received a few suggestions and interviewed a few people. This was all done a month or more before she came home. One of my friends said her daughter, Hana, was interested in helping us with Lexi. Hana lived in our neighborhood and had been on the swim team with Lexi. Her mom explained that Hana was between jobs and wanted to be Lexi's caregiver. I was worried that Lexi wouldn't listen to Hana because they were close to the same age. Summer and I discussed this when we were in Atlanta. After interviewing Hana and explaining the situation, we decided to give it a try. Hana was 22, blonde and beautiful. A bonus was she was a makeup artist, and Lexi adores makeup. Right before Lexi returned home, we found out she would be approved for Medicaid in a few weeks, and that they would pay for the caregiver if we went through an agency. During my search for a caregiver, my yoga teacher told me about another yoga student whose family owned a home health care agency. I contacted them, and they were able to hire Hana and give her the training that was required. At least that was falling into place.

In addition to therapy, I had to find a multitude of doctors. The caseworker at Shepherd Center assisted me with finding the correct doctors and making appointments. We had a lot of appointments, especially when she first was home.

I invited her friends to come over before they left for college so they would know what to expect and be able to help Lexi. We were lucky that Lexi looked fine. She had some scars, but they were not immediately noticeable. When her friends saw her, they would think she was like she was before May 19. She isn't. *She is still healing, and her friends needed to understand that.* I explained what she could and couldn't do, and how I needed them to help protect her from herself. I explained that after high school many friends go their own way, and if they couldn't be supportive, they needed to exit her life. I asked her friends to bring their parents, but only a few did. I felt I did everything I could.

In Atlanta we had been in a protective cocoon and were able to control what she did. That all changed once we were back in Virginia. She wanted her life to go on like before the crash, and that wasn't possible. It was very hard having her home and around her friends. When she came home, most of her friends were already away at college, which helped some. She had a small group of friends who were going to school locally and I tried to work with them to protect her.

I was afraid the loss of Abby would really hit her when she returned home. The counselor at Shepherd Center said she hadn't dealt with Abby's death and warned us that returning to Virginia would bring up everything. I knew the reality of losing Abby would hit her now because Abby was not associated with Atlanta—but Virginia was. Everywhere she went there would be reminders of Abby.

Dealing with Friends—Especially if the Patient is a Teen or Young Adult

This was really hard for me. Lexi is very social and independent. Because she looked "fine," I felt it was very important for her friends to understand what to expect. TBI is known as the "invisible injury" as it is unseen and unless the person has other injuries they will look "normal." Because of the legal issues I hadn't been able to communicate much to her friends. Also, we were far away so very few of her friends had seen her since the crash.

I invited many of her friends to come over to our house before she came home so I could let them know what to expect. I offered three different times to allow as many of her friends to attend as possible. Here were some of the key points of the meeting:

1. I had them put their phones in a basket, so they couldn't record what I was saying or take photos.

2. I started at her feet and went up her body to review her injuries. That was the way they explained her injuries to us at Shepherd Center.

3. Because her vision was impaired, I asked them to walk on her left side, so she didn't run into things or get hit by something she couldn't see.

4. I explained her thinking was slower, that it should improve but it may take her a while to come up with a word.

5. Her emotions were unregulated, so she may act over-emotionally or not react at all when she might be expected to react.

6. Her judgement was not where a typical 18-year-olds would be. She would say she was okay and then do something when she shouldn't. That was why I needed her friends to help protect her.

7. I explained that she could have a seizure and gave them a sheet on what to do in the event of a seizure.

8. I asked them to come to our house and hang out and play games when she first comes home instead wanting her to leave the house. If they requested it would be easier than me telling her she couldn't leave. She needs activities to help her brain make new connections.

9. I explained that caffeine, alcohol or drugs could cause a seizure.

10. I asked them to text me if they wanted to spend time with her, so I could help regulate how much time she spent with her friends in the beginning. I didn't want her to be overwhelmed.

11. TBI survivors find loud noises, large crowds, and flashing lights overwhelming so they needed to be aware of that. If she seemed overwhelmed, they needed to leave.

12. I told them that after high school everyone goes their own way, and if they couldn't handle it or be supportive, they should exit her life. I said, "She needs a wingman who can support her recovery."

Chapter 14

Home at Last

"There is no place like home."
– Dorothy in *The Wizard of Oz*

Four months and two days after Lexi walked out to go to the beach, she finally came home.

It was wonderful to all be under one roof and to see her sleeping in her own bed, which we all wanted so badly. However, it was hard because her friends wanted her to go out and Lexi would tell me, "I am 18 and can make my own decisions." Ray and I knew she couldn't make good decisions because of her injury. It became an on-going battle. We tried to compromise, but she wanted everything her way. Again, another effect of her injury. Her executive functions were not back to the level of a typical 18-year-old, which any parent could agree is not great. As my counselor told me, this was just another storm to get through.

A week after she came home she ran out of pills, and when she told me, the pharmacy was closed. I thought I had everything covered. I beat myself up that I missed her pill refill.

Our neighbor organized a meal train for dinners to be delivered a few times a week for the first month we were home, which was such a huge help. I loved coming home to a dinner that was already cooked. It was one less thing I had to worry about as we tried to transition being at home.

My work was open seven days a week, so I was off on

Sunday and Tuesday. Every Tuesday for the first couple months, we had some sort of appointment for Lexi. I remember one Tuesday we were gone for 10 hours running around to various doctors' appointments, and it was too much for her and for me too. We were both bushed.

In addition, I had to schedule other doctors' appointments, coordinate the caregivers and a million other things. Before she came home, but also after, it was an additional full-time job. I was beyond exhausted and totally stressed out.

Hana was a great caregiver because when they were out, it looked like two friends together. Right after she came home, Lexi and Hana went to our local coffee shop. Lexi and Abby had gone for coffee every morning before school and to "study." Now when Lexi arrived with Hana, the manager gave her a big hug and told her how glad she was to see her. Lexi told her she couldn't believe they stayed open without her and Abby. The manager said there were lots of other coffee lovers like her. The manager gave both Lexi and Hana free drinks. Lexi thought that was great. Before the crash Lexi would say it was her goal in life to have the barista recognize her and know what her drink was. When that happened a year or more before the crash, she was thrilled. Now, it happened for a totally different reason.

It was a challenge for both Ray and me as we needed to be home with her and drive her everywhere. With me working one weekend day and often nights until seven, a lot of this fell onto Ray.

Shepherd Center recommended we lock up all alcohol and drugs, even over-the-counter drugs. We got rid of all alcohol and bought a safe for the pills. I even locked up our extra car keys because we didn't know if Lexi would try to drive.

I have always been a worrier, but what had happened

on May 19, 2017 was exponentially worse than my wildest dream. I was much more anxious than I was before the crash. If she didn't text me back right away when she was out, I would have an anxiety attack. I especially had a hard time when she went to the beach the summer of 2018. It is her happy place, but I was a mess when she was there. I especially didn't want her going back to the same beach she had been to on the day of the crash or driving by the crash site.

She was very emotional and angry, especially at me. I was warned most of her anger would be directed at me, and it was. Although she was also like that before the crash, her anger was much, much worse. It was a difficult time. I would try to get her to do yoga, meditation, and other things to control her emotions, but she didn't listen. I always say it is hard enough having an 18- or 19-year-old; add a traumatic brain injury on top, *and it is pure hell.*

I have an acquaintance who experienced a tragedy in her life, so I had contacted her for a referral to a counselor who deals in trauma. Before Lexi came home, I was seeing this counselor on a semi-regular basis. It was hard to fit in my schedule, but I did my best. I took Lexi to see her with me once she was home, and even Ray went once. She helped me put things in perspective and diagnosed me with post-traumatic stress disorder (PTSD). She suggested I take an anti-depressant for a short time to help me not only sleep but regulate my emotions. I did and it helped me deal with what I was going through. I am not one to take an aspirin for a headache unless it is bad, but I really needed help to navigate through everything.

After Lexi returned home, she continued physical, occupational and speech therapy at our local hospital three days a week. I wanted to keep down the time we needed the caregivers, so I would drop Lexi off on my way to work and the caregiver would pick her up after therapy. Getting her out the door in the mornings was harder than it was before the crash, but eventually it became easier. Her sense of time was way off. I had to tell her to be ready a half-hour before I wanted to leave. At our first appointment with the occupational therapist, I asked if they had swimming therapy. She laughed and said no, explaining that at Shepherd Center we had been at a five-star hotel, and now we were at a two-star hotel, a nice two-star hotel, but still a two-star hotel. I thought that was so funny, true, but funny. Instead of five hours of therapy five days a week, it was now three hours of therapy two to three times a week.

Once we returned home we all became sick. I was amazed with all the stress we had been under, the various hospitals we were in, and airplanes we had been on, none of us had become sick before. I guess it was our bodies saying, okay, now is the time.

Lexi wanted a different counselor than mine and I found one she liked. She only went a few times; she always had one excuse or another. I was trying to get her to go back. I told her to go while I was paying, but so far it hadn't worked. I couldn't believe anyone could handle what Lexi had been though, with the changes to her life, and the loss of Abby, without help.

She needed to do so many ordinary things once we returned home. We couldn't brush her teeth while she was in the coma. Once she was awake, I would help her brush, but it was a good month or more before she did a good job. She didn't wear her retainer until we were at Shepherd Center. Once she started wearing it again her teeth hurt, but the retainer still fit. One of the first appointments she had was with our dentist. We were all shocked that she didn't have any cavities. She was very happy that she was given a custom bleach kit to whiten her teeth.

She needed to have her hair roots touched up. Our wonderful hair stylist Annette came in on a Sunday when the salon was closed to do Lexi's hair. It was the one place I was comfortable leaving her because Annette knew what to do in the event of a seizure, because of her husband's brain tumor. I was terrified about the possibility of a seizure. Due to all the anesthesia she had, her hair was much thinner, requiring Annette to be careful with the color. Annette assured us her hair would grow back. Lexi felt much better after her hair was done.

Day 131: Tuesday, September 26

The orthopedist in Atlanta had suggested I try to find a surgeon to repair Lexi's arm at a teaching hospital in Virginia since we wanted to get home. I asked my therapist who is on the staff of a teaching hospital, she suggested a doctor at University of Virginia (UVA). I contacted his office. He came highly recommended by numerous people. I had sent the x-rays and CAT scan to him before we went to see him. UVA is a three-hour drive each way. I scheduled the appointment for the first Tuesday after she came home. Because they set up an appointment after seeing her records, both Lexi and I were expecting good news. We talked on the way up about where we would stay during the surgery, and what we would do for follow-up appointments.

When we met with the doctor it was not what we expected. He was adamant that the surgery was very high risk and not worth it because she would have limited movement. If it didn't work, it would have to be fused again and maybe even amputated. I asked him if it was his daughter if he would do it, and he said no. I was crying in his office. We were both very disappointed and upset. We had been given such hope and that was now dashed.

The only good thing about the long drive to Charlottesville was we took her friend Katie to lunch.

Day 140: Thursday, October 5

I took this day off to go to the District Attorney's Office. It was the first time I had been there. The next day there would be a hearing and they needed me to testify that Lexi has life-altering injuries. I saw Liz, the witness, again and met her daughter. In a weird six degrees of separation, her daughter went to eighth grade with Emma, Lexi's friend. I spoke to the Davises; then I was able to leave as the driver's attorney said he would accept the fact that Lexi has permanent injuries. I could have attended the hearing, but I didn't want to be in the same room with the driver. I read about the hearing online and Liz's testimony how Lexi was breathing as if she was dying. Luckily, I was alone as I sobbed again.

One of her friends came over and showed me a post from some moron who went to school in Virginia Beach and didn't know either girl, defending the driver. I was livid! Another level of this hell. A lot of both girls' friends had responded to this jerk who had wanted to seem important.

She was often acting like a young child with full-on tantrums. She was also insulting us, and every little thing was a huge fight. This was so bad, even worse than I had imagined.

I decided to Lexi her have a sleepover with her friends. I talked to the girls about not staying up late because Lexi needed to sleep, but they didn't listen. She wanted to start driving with her friends and that terrified me. She told me the night of the sleepover was the first time she had felt normal.

Day 155: Friday, October 20

Yesterday was five months—and I am so close to the edge I am barely functioning. It is surprising I am even upright, let alone holding onto my job. Earlier this week I was up at five a.m. and baked a cake. Yesterday, Ray asked me where the cake was. I had left it in the oven. Thank God I had turned off the oven and didn't burn down the house.

Lexi loved to perform and didn't shy away from the spotlight before, but now the attention due to the crash was uncomfortable for her. She never really saw the love and support we received from our community because she was in the hospital and has no memory of that time. I was hoping that it had been long enough the story would have died down, but it hit the media again with the driver's court appearance right before she came home. One day she went out to dinner with a friend and a woman came up to her and asked if she was Lexi. When she said yes, the lady said she had been praying for her and asked her if she could give her a hug as she was a mom. She of course, said yes. At Lexi's new primary care doctor appointment, I went in and the nurse told me she knew who Lexi was and started to cry. I can't imagine how hard all of this was for her. One of her friends told her she *was the girl that lived*, like Harry Potter was the boy who lived.

Last week we all went to the Navy Ball. Ray and I had been to the Ball the previous year, and I called it the adult prom. Lexi had missed her prom, so Ray wanted to take her and a friend. We bought the crazy expensive dress that I wouldn't let her buy for her senior prom. It had a large skirt like Cinderella. She and Hana had taken it to get altered. The night of the ball she told me the dress was too big on the top, and it was strapless. I tried to tape it, but didn't have the correct tape and we were leaving in 15 minutes. Then she mentioned the alternations lady had asked her if she wanted the top taken in and she had said no. Note to self: don't let a TBI patient get alterations without you. I had the hair and makeup people come to the house and do our makeup and hair. Lexi looked so lovely; it made me cry to see her. We took her friend Emma with us. When we were getting out of the elevator at the hotel where the ball was being held, there was a mom with her two small kids. She said to her kids, "Wait until the princess gets off." Ellie and David were there as well, and despite the stress of Lexi having to pull up her dress all the time, it was a great evening. It didn't make up for missing her senior prom, but it was the best we could do.

In mid-October she was complaining about her arm, and it looked like the pins were about to poke through her skin. The skin on her arm was very, very thin. I called her arm surgeon and he got her in right away. The x-ray showed her bones were healed, and the pins were indeed coming out. The doctor was amazed at how well she was doing. He told me it made his day to see her. He told her she was in a "dark place" the last time he saw her. He had been a trauma surgeon for 30 years and had never fused an elbow before. They scheduled the surgery for the first available time. This would be her fourth surgery. It was a very hard surgery for her. She was in incredible pain and pain medicine didn't work and made her feel sick. The surgery was outpatient, and that first night she was in so much pain I wished they had kept her overnight in the hospital. She didn't even eat anything for three days. I was concerned because she missed all therapy and the hyperbaric chamber treatments that she had started the week before.

To help her feel "normal," I let her go out for dinner with her friends. One of her friend's moms drove them because I didn't want her going that far with her friends driving. I told her I would pick them up at seven p.m. when I was off work. At 6:30 I started calling and texting her from work. When she didn't answer the phone or return my texts, I tried to control my panic and left work and came home after a long day. Right after I arrived home, she called and wanted to be picked up. Ray wanted to go get her, but I wanted her home sooner because it was a half hour away. We had an Uber driver go get them. I was so upset that she hadn't responded to my texts or calls. I was trying to help her be the old Lexi and give her some freedom, but then something like that happened.

Day 162: Friday, October 27

We were continuing to adapt to all of us being home but didn't quite have a rhythm yet; hopefully soon. She was improving with the therapy she was getting here. It was not as fast as it was in Atlanta, but we did see improvements.

I was still so spacey that Lexi would ask me often, "Who has the brain injury mom?"

Ellie, her sister, goes all out for Halloween because she has kids. She chooses a theme and the entire family participates. Lexi had never participated because she had other things to do, but this year, she would go trick-or-treating with all of us. I was really looking forward to that.

Day 185: Sunday, November 19

Six months ago, my world imploded. Ray, Marshall and I were talking last night about how far she had come. We were told the first six months we would see exponential growth. After that it would continue but be slower. Now was the end of the "golden time." I was comfortable in that I had done everything I could for her in such a short time. She had improved a lot, but no matter what I did, she was not the same as she was before the crash. I know she will always be different, and I continue to grieve for what we all have lost. I would give anything to turn back time.

Her friends were now home for Thanksgiving. I knew

this would be a challenge and it was. Thursday night she wanted to have a Friendsgiving at our house because her friends' parents had said no. I said okay after she told me it would only be a maximum of 12 people. When I got home, she told me she wanted us to leave the house for the entire night and that 50 people would be there. I never would have allowed that before the crash. When I told her no, she became hysterical and said, "If I can't live, then I should have died in the crash." That almost killed me. She kept saying it was "her" health. It was, but I had to explain to her she couldn't be expected to make good decisions yet.

Marshall had to tell her "No" the other day, and she reacted the same with him. We couldn't reason with her, and she was violent. She would kick and hit us. I knew it was the brain injury, but it didn't make it any easier. It was like having a small child in an adult's body.

Day 202: Wednesday, December 6 – Mayo Clinic

When she had the pins removed, I talked to her surgeon and explained that the surgeon in Atlanta thought he could give her movement but couldn't do the surgery before we came home due to her heart infection. Then I related what happened at the University of Virginia and asked him for his opinion. He suggested I contact a doctor at the Mayo Clinic. He had to send a referral to get Lexi seen. I had been calling and following up for months with no response. Finally, on Monday, November 27, I got a letter saying we had a two-day appointment starting Wednesday, December 6—*in nine days*. When Mayo says you have an appointment, you go. I booked flights costing over $1,400 with such short notice, and we flew up that morning. Sometimes I too forget that Lexi has a brain injury. At the airport, she went to the bathroom and I didn't walk with her. When it was a while before she came back, I asked her what had taken her so long. She said she couldn't find the bathroom, even though it was close to where we were, and there were signs. *I can't let my guard down.*

The Mayo Hospital in Rochester, Minnesota was a fantastic place. There were heated tunnels underground with carpet and beautiful art work that connected all the hospital buildings and the hotels. It was gigantic. After we went to the main check-in, Lexi then had to get her blood drawn. The waiting room for the blood draw holds about 300 people, but we got in quickly. People from all over the world were there, with different languages being spoken. After the blood draw, we went up to the orthopedic center. Neither of us was expecting the doctor to be able to give her any movement based on the meeting we had with the UVA doctor. My goal for this trip was to get her in the Mayo system so if surgical advancements came up in the future, they would contact us. First, we told the assisting doctor the story. Then the main doctor came in and we told the story again. He told us he thought he might be able to give her some movement. It was based on whether there was enough bone left to attach a piece of cadaver tissue to. He felt she had enough muscle left. She told him she really wanted to be able to lick her fingers. *The things we take for granted.* He explained that the surgery would only last about five to seven years, but it could be repeated if necessary. He said he might have to do a skin graft from her thigh because her skin was very thin. I offered to give her some of my skin and they could do a tummy tuck along the way. He laughed and said that I was not the first mom to offer that. He ordered an MRI and a CAT scan. They could fit her in for a CAT scan the following morning, but the MRI machine was booked until the next Monday. They told us she could have the MRI back home. We both walked out of there in shock. We had not expected any possibility of surgery.

After she had the CAT scan, we left the hospital the next morning. We had an extra half-day, so we spent the day at the Mall of America near the Minneapolis airport. She loved the mall, and we had a great time together. I bought her a few things, and we had a nice dinner, then went to bed as our flight was early the next morning. When booking the flight, I chose to go through Atlanta. It was December and I didn't want to risk a snowstorm. I checked before we left the hotel, and the flight was on time. By the time we arrived at the airport, the flight was delayed due to a large snowstorm . . . in Atlanta. Our original flight was scheduled for 10 a.m. but we didn't leave until about one p.m. I was worried about making our connecting flight in Atlanta. Both my son and Ray were calling us and trying to figure out what to do. When we arrived in Atlanta, all the hotels were booked and everything was shut down. I even texted our Atlanta friend Gia, but she was out in the suburbs at her cousin's, so we couldn't stay with her. It was looking like we were going to have to sleep in the airport. Finally, we boarded the plane about 6:30 p.m. The pilot kept going in circles around the airport waiting to get de-iced.

While reading Facebook, I saw a story in the local paper about how the Davises had filed a $32 million lawsuit. Lexi was sitting in the row behind me. I was quietly sobbing as I read the article. None of this should be happening. No lawsuits. No Mayo Clinic. Both girls should be going to school at Virginia Tech. None of this was fair.

After all of the pilot's circling, we had to go back to the gate to get more gas. We finally took off about 11 p.m. and landed in Virginia about midnight. Having woken up at six a.m., we were both exhausted. I was really glad to be home, but I had to be at work in a few hours.

A few weeks later, after the MRI was done, the Mayo doctor called and said he could do the surgery because Lexi had enough bone left. However, there was a high risk she would be in constant pain—and she wasn't in any pain now. I talked to the doctor twice, and my million-dollar question for every doctor was: What would you do if it were your daughter? He told me he would wait and see what she wants to do in the future. It didn't make a difference if we have the surgery done this year or in five years. Ultimately, it was up to Lexi, but I didn't think it was worth it.

Day 220: Sunday, December 24 – Christmas Eve

A few weeks ago, a unicorn ornament appeared on my kitchen table. I thought Lexi picked it up when she was out with her caregiver. When I finally asked her about it, she said she didn't get it, and she didn't know where it came from. At Halloween I had seen a post from Abby's mom about Abby's Halloween costume that was a unicorn and how much she loved that costume. I finally asked Ray about it and he said the staff had given it to him when he had been at the craft store. He almost threw it out as he left the store, but didn't and brought it home. I felt it was another sign from Abby.

On Christmas Eve, I finally went to Abby's grave for only the second time and took the unicorn ornament. I cried and cried. I talk to Abby when I go to her grave. When I got back home, Ray knew something was wrong. I can't help but think how lucky we were that we are not visiting a gravesite. I told Lexi where I had been and she said nothing. I was very afraid for her because she must deal with all of this at some time.

Day 232: January 5, 2018

It was the start of a new year, and although I was sick, we had taken Lexi and two friends down to the Outer Banks of North Carolina. We wanted her out of town for New Year's because every day with her friend's home from school was hard. She was constantly sending me nasty texts to leave her alone. She was so incredibly rude to Ray and me. Right after we got home from the Outer Banks, she and her brother, Marshall went down to Universal Studios in Florida. Again, we wanted to get her out of town, but we couldn't afford to keep this up.

Being a caregiver for anyone with a brain injury was very difficult because your responsibilities were never ending. The family dynamics change, and it was very stressful. I am not a very patient person, and have never been, so this was very hard for me. I don't know what I would have done if I hadn't had Ray. Lexi was a typical teenager before the crash and, yes, we fought. I have always told my kids they know how to push my buttons because they installed them. I am my kids' parent, not their friend. They have plenty of friends. I am strict. My motto is *trust but verify*. Lexi was mad because I would periodically reach out to her friends' parents to make sure she was at their house or going to their house.

Now I felt like I was wound up so tight I could snap at any moment.

I remember talking to Aunt Jamie shortly after the crash, and she said I was the most protective parent she knew. The irony is that Lexi wouldn't wear a helmet with her bike, so I gave the bike away so she wouldn't fall and get a head injury. I had told Lexi I didn't want her driving in anyone's car that didn't have side air bags because I know how important they are to safety in the event of a crash.

Lexi is headstrong and independent. She was ready to go to college when senior year started. We fought a lot that senior year. I remember talking to my friend who has a daughter the same age about the struggle it was to let them become more independent as they separate from us.

I remember a similar thing happening with my son. I had lunch a few months ago with Kristen, and we talked about how we wanted to raise strong daughters, but we didn't plan on them being *so strong willed with us.*

Day 250: Tuesday January 23

A few months ago, when the police department's fatal crash investigator brought Lexi's phone back, he finally met her. The phone was filthy, but it worked. As much as she had threatened for months to yell at the police, she didn't. The officer showed us the six-inch file he had on the crash and answered any questions we had. I know the police worked so hard on this case. They wanted the driver to get the maximum sentence possible. I will always be so appreciative of everything they have done.

The officer had submitted Lexi for an award for wearing her seat belt. If she hadn't had her seatbelt on, she would have been killed. She had "won" the award, and today was the day we were going to get it. About twenty police officers were there as well as some of the people from the prosecutor's office. The police department's chaplain was there. I had met him at the hospital and he had called a few times and had sent her a beautiful card. When he spoke at the ceremony, he talked about how they didn't think she would make it through the first night. It was like I heard that for the first time. I sobbed again; it was like my heart was being ripped out. She was given a plaque and flowers. I was happy for us to meet the hard-working police officers who worked on the crash. I had invited the witnesses. After the ceremony we were given a tour of the station: it was a special event. I felt bad because I told Ray he didn't need to come as I was not expecting it to be such a big deal. He would have loved the tour.

Day 262: Monday, February 5

A few days ago, Lexi celebrated her birthday. She spent all day with her friends and the night at a hotel at the beach. I was totally against it, but the girls paid so there was nothing I could do. I was worried and so relieved when she came home. She did sleep most of the day, as likely they hadn't slept the night before.

She was so angry all the time, especially with me. Yesterday, she told me I reminded her of the crash all the time—and what she can't do. I was simply trying to get her to be realistic and to take it easy. I felt like I couldn't do anything right around her.

She wanted us to drive her all the time and we were supposed to drop everything to take her wherever. After she and Ray had a blow up yesterday, she and I got into it. She wanted to go tanning and I didn't want her to get on a tanning bed. She didn't need more risk of cancer after all she had been through.

Day 332: Monday, April 16

I was now unemployed. When I accepted the job, I knew I would have to work a few nights and one weekend day. I think if the crash hadn't happened, we could have made it work. However, with Lexi home and always needing someone to drive her, it was too much for both Ray and me. My employer was having mandatory training the day the criminal trial for the driver was scheduled. I explained to my boss that I needed to attend the trial, so she asked me if I could go testify and then come in to work. Well, no, I couldn't do that. I needed to attend every minute of the trial to make sure the jerk who did this gets everything he deserves. With that request, I saw the writing on the wall. A few weeks later when I missed Easter with our family to work, Ray said I needed to find another job. I had had two other companies writing me offers when I had accepted that job, so I contacted both. I accepted the first one who responded. As much as I loved my job, I couldn't make it work for my family.

I had a month off before the new company wanted me to start. We were all going to Utah in early May for a treatment for Lexi. It was during this month off I felt I was finally able to decompress. The first Sunday I was unemployed Ray and I drove to see our grandkids; he told me that I was a different woman. He said my smile was back and I was the woman he fell in love with. I didn't realize how much all the pressure had affected me.

I made every moment of the month I had off count. I spent a lot of time with friends, which I hadn't been able to do recently. I was able to work out and just be in the moment. I needed to find time to breathe and find some happiness again.

Lexi had a boyfriend that we really liked. He seemed to be helping smooth out her emotions. She was a little easier to live with now.

Chapter 15

School: Community College

"Education is not the filling of a pail, but the lighting of a fire."
– William Butler Yeats

In December, Lexi finished with physical and occupational therapy. Her speech therapist said she couldn't do much more to prepare her for school; she needed to be in a real class. She compared Lexi's cognitive abilities to someone who has had multiple concussions. Shepherd Center had told us she probably wouldn't be able to start school until the fall of 2018, and then only one on-line class. I found out about a program at Boston University where they were doing a study to see how TBI students could learn effectively. It would include lots of one-on-one coaching and study strategies. The program was free, but we would have had to live in downtown Boston for four months. I figured it would be at least $20,000 to cover housing, and I would have had to give up my job. We applied to the program, and Lexi was accepted. I wanted to give her any advantage we could, but it didn't really make sense with the cost.

After much thought and research, we decided to pass on Boston and enroll her in our local community college. She had taken an AP Biology class her senior year, so we signed her up for essentially the same class at the community college. I spoke to her speech therapist and the researchers in Boston, and they both agreed it was a good alternative. If the community college classes were too hard, then she could get into the next session at Boston University. Lexi agreed to this: we always tried to include her in the decision-making. Her AP Biology teacher offered to help her with the community college class if she needed it. We met with the community college disability office and, even though she hadn't had her neuropsychic test done, they put accommodations in place for her. These would include extra time for tests, sitting on the left side of classroom so she could see the board, access to the teacher's notes, and the ability to record the lectures. We also decided to sign her up for a short-term anatomy class that included only eight weeks of new material. She wanted to be a doctor before the crash, and still wants to be one.

She was such a science nerd. She told me her biology professor told science jokes and she was the only one in her community college class who laughed. We were taking small steps to get her back to school.

Chapter 16

Remembering Abby

"There are some who bring a light so great to the world that even after they are gone the light remains."
– Unknown

Before she returned home from Atlanta, Lexi talked about wanting to do something to remember Abby. We discussed various options, including a picnic table in the senior garden at the high school. I liked that idea, but wanted more of a public place. We decided on a bench at a local garden. I knew Abby's senior photos were taken there, and after we made the decision, I found out the Davises had spent Mother's Day there in 2016. I started a crowd-sourcing page to raise money for the bench. Lexi and I went to the gardens to choose a place for it. Lexi wanted the bench near the water because Abby loved the beach. We wanted to dedicate the bench on the one-year anniver-sary. I figured this would be a good way to memorialize the day for everyone.

On April 30, Lexi finally went to see the Davises. She went with her friend, Nathan, who was also a good friend of Abby. I had wanted Abby's family to come to our house. This would allow us to be there to protect Lexi and not to have all the memories of Abby at her house. Of course, she didn't take my advice. Lexi and Nathan went out for dinner and then went to the Davis' home at 7:30 pm. I was anxious about this meeting. As I have explained, Abby looked very much like her mom, Terri. About 10:30 I texted Nathan to see if he was with Lexi because when I texted her, she wasn't responding—*a huge trigger for my anxiety*. Nathan texted me back at 11:10 p.m. and said they were just leaving the Davis' home. It was Good Friday.

Abby's mom posted on-line how powerful it was seeing Lexi again. She said it was like hugging Abby again, and how it gave her a small amount of peace seeing, talking, and holding her. She said, "Seeing her alive is like seeing a miracle of God. I know Abby was happy we were finally able to meet again. For the first time in 11 long months, I'm crying tears of hope. Lexi will now live for them both, going on to do great things with this second chance at life, and her friend Abby, my beautiful, amazing, intelligent, kind daughter, will truly be at peace and will always be with her. This is just the first step along my journey of healing, but it couldn't have come at a better time than Easter."

Chapter 17

The One-Year Anniversary

"When you come to the end of your rope, tie a knot and hang on."
– Franklin D. Roosevelt

I had been dreading the one-year anniversary. The 19th of every month is a bad day, so I knew that May 19th was going to be horrible. When I tried to talk to Lexi about it, she would shut me down, and I was worried about how she was handling this.

Abby's mom, grandma, and I had met with the garden about the bench placement in April. We had discussed having their priest come and do a quick prayer as a dedication. The gardens didn't want a large group there unless we rented space. I tried to encourage everyone to keep it small. I had wanted the dedication to be at two p.m., but the Davises wanted to be at the crash site at 3:19, the time of the crash. I deferred to them, so we set the dedication for noon. When we arrived at the garden, the Davis family was already there. Their priest had another commitment so we didn't hold a dedication. Ray and I were there with all our kids. Lexi had invited a few of her and Abby's close friends. Rain was forecasted and threatening, but it held off until we drove away. Another sign from Abby?

The local paper sent a reporter who I had talked to

previously. He had called me the day before and told me the Davises had invited him. I didn't know if Lexi would talk to him, but I told him we would be there. I was looking forward to finally meeting him. Lexi did speak to him, and the photographer took a photo of her tattoo in Abby's memory. In the article, the Davises talked about how the bench gave them peace.

The bench was in a beautiful spot near the rose garden where Abby had her senior photos taken. It has since been moved to its permanent spot in a new garden still close to the water but overlooking the rose garden.

The anniversary was emotional for me. Because Lexi wouldn't talk about the crash, I wrote her a letter telling her how far she had come, and how proud I was of her. She later told me she read the letter, and thanked me for everything I had done to help her. Maybe she had a small inkling of some of what Ray and I have been through.

Chapter 18

Lexi's a Virginia Tech Hokie

*"Every driven person comes from a mountain
of pain they wish to keep hidden."*
– Chris Colfer

From the very beginning, our goal was to get Lexi to college. Everything from Shepherd Center on was laser focused on meeting that goal. We took small steps to get her back to school.

When we returned home from Shepherd Center, I begged her to choose a college closer to home. I love Virginia Tech (VT), but Blacksburg is a long drive from our house. That town also gets a lot of snow, and I am terrified of her slipping and falling and hurting her head. But no, my girl wanted to be a Virginia Tech Hokie. When she was doing well at community college, we discovered that Tech offered a summer academy program that is limited to 300 students. We all agreed this would be a good next step. They have various tracks the students can take, including a pre-med track. This was an opportunity to live on campus, eat in the dining halls and go to classes. Tech normally has about 30,000 students, so in comparison, even with various summer camps, and the Corp of Cadets and student athletes there, the campus was relatively empty. This would give her a chance to learn her way around campus without it being packed with students. The classes were small; with only eight students, but were condensed and quite intense.

Before she left for Tech, we finally had a party in her honor. At first, she didn't want the attention, but I wanted a celebration, and when I reminded her, she might get some gifts, she was all for it. We invited everyone who would have been at her graduation party, plus some of the medical team and her attorney. It was super-hot outside, so everyone had to stay inside and our home was packed. Ray made her a fabulous VT cake and smoked BBQ. It was great to share her progress with the people we love and those who had helped her in many ways.

She had so much stuff to take to school that we had to take two cars. Marshall, Ray, Lexi and I all drove out to Blacksburg. We were amazed she fit everything into her small dorm room. It was *quite stressful* moving her in, so when it came time to say goodbye, it was surprisingly easy. After Marshall left to go home, Ray and I went out to have a beer and celebrate being empty nesters at last.

Lexi loved summer academy. When she took her first test, she called to say it was hard even though she had studied a lot. I consoled her and told her she now knew what a college test was like, and she would do better next time. A few hours later, she texted me that she had received an 87, the highest in her class. What a gigantic accomplishment for her. We were all proud. She ended up earning As in all her classes.

When Marshall picked her up after summer academy, he had to move her to her fall dorm across the courtyard. She video called us when she had finally moved into her fall dorm. She was showing us the room and the "miniscule" closet. She had no room for all her shoes, so she asked us if we could get her another room that she could use for a closet. We laughed so hard. We told her she was a princess, and she responded that she was a "humble princess." We haven't laughed that hard in a long time.

Lexi was home for four days between summer and fall classes. During that time, she had to get her hair colored, go see the prosecutors, and go to many doctors' appointments. I was working, but Ray had recently retired, so he took her to the appointments. He had a new appreciation of what I went through for the months after she was home from Atlanta. While she was home, I asked if she was as happy at Tech as she thought she would be, and she told me she was even happier. She wanted to spend as much time with her dog, Harley, as she could when she was home. Her smile was worth all the work the dog caused.

Chapter 19

Dealing with the Legal System

"Tough times never last, but strong people do."
– Robert H. Schuller

When something like this happens, you may be thrown into the legal world, both civil and criminal, as we were. As soon as you can, hire a good lawyer. Lexi's crash happened on a Friday at 3:19 p.m. and I hired an attorney on Monday at noon. This is another place you need to use your resources—ask friends, other professionals, and ask on Facebook for recommendations. That Sunday after the crash when I talked to Abby's parents, we discussed hiring a shared attorney, and because they were so overwhelmed, they said they'd defer to me.

When I hired the attorney the following Monday, I asked him about sharing an attorney with the Davises, and he explained that we need to have separate attorneys, so each attorney was looking after their own clients. I passed along some references he had given me to Abby's family. I had control over few things, but I was happy with my decision. It has turned out to be a much longer relationship than I had anticipated.

I had to go to court and get a guardianship because Lexi was 18. This would give me legal standing to make decisions both medical and financial for her. A Guardian ad Litem was also assigned. It was his job to be her advocate with the court on whether she was able to handle her affairs. We needed to move the court date until I was back from Atlanta, allowing me to attend. It was difficult emotionally for me to go to court to get the guardianship because I knew Lexi would be angry, but it was for the best. A key aspect of a guardianship is you need to provide an accounting for all financial accounts. Tracking her money was not an issue until she was home and I'd give her some cash. After struggling through the first few reports, I gave her a monthly allowance with a gift card, which made it much easier to balance the report that the court required. Be sure to check the rules if you must provide a report.

If there is a criminal element to an accident, you will also get to know the prosecutors. Initially, the prosecutors told us it would be about a year before the driver went to trial. Before there is a trial, there are many court appearances. I didn't go to the early court appearances. The Davises went, but I couldn't be in the same room with the driver. He had the guts to ask to be released on bond, but it was denied. The preliminary hearing was set for early October. I didn't go to that either.

The driver ended up pleading guilty 347 days after he chose to drink and do drugs and then drive a fully loaded delivery truck. I was glad we didn't have to undergo a criminal trial. When he pled guilty, both Ray and I went to court. Lexi wanted nothing to do with anything associated with the crash, so she wasn't there. This was the first time I would be in the same room with him. There was quite a large crowd. Before the driver came in to plead guilty, he drew it out to make it even harder on the families. The attorneys had warned us this could happen, but eventually he entered the courtroom and admitted his guilt. I glanced over at him but couldn't look at him. I looked out the window and cried as he admitted to the pain he had caused us and so many others.

Very few people know about subrogation; I certainly didn't. This is the definition from Google: "In the event of an insurance claim, 'subrogation' refers to the process by which your insurance company collects money from the party at fault (or their insurance company) to recover funds, you or your insurance company have already paid, including your deductible." It is a federal law buried in a law that deals with retirement benefits. If there is an accident with any kind of settlement, and your company is self-funded or government-based, the medical insurance company wants to be reimbursed.

Remember, Ray and I got married when we did so Lexi would have multiple insurances. We had my insurance with my former employer, which I was under because I had just switched jobs; my insurance with my new employer; the insurance through Ray's employer; and his military coverage. As a result, we had lots of insurance companies to negotiate with. The furniture company had only $1 million in insurance coverage, and *we had over $1 million in just medical bills*. That didn't include travel costs, treatments not covered by insurance, or co-payments. Lexi will have a lifetime of medical costs due to the crash. There are two families and two attorneys to split the money between. Our attorney has said it would have been better if Lexi didn't have any medical insurance coverage, but then she wouldn't have been able to get into Shepherd Center. We tried to do what was right and make sure she was covered and that everyone would get paid.

I was the only one who had medical coverage on my auto insurance of $7,000, and because I had two cars on my insurance, it was doubled to $14,000. The attorneys sent to my auto insurer copies of the bills Lexi had accrued, and they put that money in a trust to use. This money allowed us to pay the co-pays and some of her other treatments that weren't covered by insurance. Be sure to check into this. For some reason, no one else involved in the crash had auto insurance with medical coverage. Make sure you have that. God forbid you need it, but it is worth it if you do.

Initially, both families' attorneys were working together. The Davises had hired one of the attorneys that mine recommended. After a few months they changed their attorney and their new attorney wasn't as willing to work with ours. In September when our attorney called and asked if I wanted to sue the furniture store and the driver, I said YES! So, we filed suit, and our case was set for a year later. He was happy to get a date that soon due to the court's backlog.

At the end of May 2018, I was notified that the furniture company's insurance wanted us to participate in a mediation to review both lawsuits. The mediation would be confidential and was not binding —meaning that if we did not resolve the case in mediation, we would still be able to try the cases before a jury. We were told that mediation was the best shot to get the most money. A trial would be expensive, because we would need to pay many of her doctors to testify, plus the court fees. Both families had to agree to this. At the end of August 2018, we met at our attorney's office. We were spread out in three different conference rooms over two floors. Ray, Marshall, and I were in one room; the Davises and their attorney were in another room; and the furniture company owner and his insurance company's attorney were in another room.

It was an extremely long day, from nine a.m. to five p.m. The mediator was a retired judge. I hate every aspect of the crash and I wished I could be like Lexi and ignore everything—but that wasn't an option. The judge was kind and gave us what I felt was great advice. With all of us in separate rooms, the judge was going back and forth. The starting point: How much would the furniture company owner pay? The judge asked me how much I thought was reasonable, and I told him no amount of money will bring Abby back or make Lexi whole the way she was when she woke up the morning of the 19th. But I wanted his life to change in a negative way, so I said $1 million per family. We had sued for $28 million, and the Davises had sued for $32 million. I knew that we wouldn't get that kind of money, but for both families *it was a statement on what we had lost.*

The judge returned to us and shared that the furniture company would only offer a minor settlement and they wouldn't budge beyond that.

The fly in the ointment with splitting the money between Lexi and the Davises were the liens due to Lexi's health care costs. Because of subrogation, the health insurance companies get paid back from any settlement. This is outrageous. Why do I pay for health insurance? This pissed me off to no end. I have written letters to my senators saying I would be willing to testify about the unfairness of this law.

The settlement amount was miniscule after our attorneys and the medical bills were paid. No amount of money was enough for what both families had been through and will continue to endure. Before we left, the furniture company's lawyer came upstairs to see us. He said how sorry he was for what we had been through. He explained he didn't get to choose his clients as he was a representative from the insurance company. I thought that was very nice. The owner of the furniture company has never offered us any kind of apology.

We discussed the upcoming sentencing with the mediation judge. He had sat on the bench for a long time, and he told us with the sentencing guidelines of 4–11 years total, the most we could expect was 20–30 years. Both families' attorneys had said the same thing, so we were steeling ourselves for that.

Eighteen months and two days after the crash, Lexi was home from school for Thanksgiving, and we had a court date to remove the guardianship. She was well enough to be able to handle the limited funds she had. We had to be at court at 8:30 a.m. so she could meet with the attorney before the hearing. Court started at nine a.m. When she came downstairs to leave, she wore a romper, which is basically shorts and a tank top. It was the end of November and about 40 degrees outside. I told her she needed to change, but she thought she was just fine. I said she was going to court to show she could make good decisions, and being dressed like that wouldn't help. Ray told me to back off, so I did.

When we arrived at the court, before she went through security, the sheriff told me she wasn't going to be allowed in court dressed like that. I asked the sheriff to please tell her that. Luckily Ray was there because he needed to sign some papers, so he took her home. The lawyer was freaking out because she wasn't there. I explained to our lawyer why she had to go home, who said, "Let's not bring that up to the judge." I didn't have my phone while I was in court, but when I tried to call Ray from the attorney's phone, he didn't answer. Then I was freaking out. Fortunately, court started late so Lexi made it before the judge arrived. Once she was sworn in, the attorney asked her to describe the crash. She said how she and Abby were coming back from the beach when they were hit head-on by a drunk driver. She explained how Abby was killed, and she was seriously injured. She teared up, and I was crying as well. She answered the questions from her attorney and explained to the judge that she was in school full time. Apparently, it was the same judge who granted the guardianship. I didn't recognize him because I was in a state of shock when we went to court the first time. He told her he was glad she was doing well and removed the guardianship. This will certainly make both our lives easier.

Chapter 20

Finally...Justice

"The dead cannot cry out for justice.
It is the duty of the living to do so for them."
– Lois McMaster Bujold

The driver pled guilty to all charges, but we had yet to have a sentencing hearing. I'm sure it is different in every state, but in Virginia the victims get to write a victim's impact statement to submit to the court. There are strict guidelines about what can be in the statement, and who can write one. It must be someone who had direct or financial impact. At one point we thought the girls' friends and other community members could write a letter, but after posting on Facebook, the prosecutor called me and said we couldn't do that. Only if you who had a direct impact, can you write a statement, but you cannot say what sentence you think the person should get. Nonetheless many people wrote impact statements and sent them to the families to get to the judge.

I worked on my victim impact statement for a few weeks. It was incredibly difficult, and I cried a boatload of tears. I wanted to make sure it was short and impactful. It helped in some ways that I had been working on this book, so I remembered in a way I wouldn't have without it. If you are writing a victim-impact statement and have notes, this is a good time to review them. Two days before the hearing, I had to finish my statement. It was simply too hard, and it would never be perfect. I looked at it as the most important sales pitch of my life. I wanted to let the judge know the impact this had on me, my family, and most importantly, Lexi.

The prosecutors originally wanted Lexi to do a video recording of her statement. I encouraged her because this would be her only opportunity to talk to the court—and she could speak for both her and Abby. She refused, and I had to respect her feelings. When she was home for four days between summer academy and fall semester, we went to the prosecutor's office and talked to them. She asked them who else would see her statement. She was told that only the judge, defense attorney, and prosecuting attorneys would see it. She said that she didn't want me to see it. When we came home, I wanted her to get it done before she went back to school. She was in her room, and when I asked her something, she snapped at me, saying that she was working on her statement and had emailed it in.

Ray worked on his statement the weekend before the hearing. His was very powerful, but short and sweet. I read it once it was done. Again, I cried and cried. He talked about how I was once quick to laugh, but now I was much more guarded.

Ellie sent me hers, and I cried hysterically. I hadn't thought much about the effect this had on other people before, so the statement brought it into focus. Ellie told me she cried while she was writing it.

The hearing was scheduled for a Monday. The night before, I woke up at one a.m. and couldn't go back to sleep. The hearing was supposed to start at nine a.m. We arrived about 8:30. I had kept the voicemail her friend had left to tell me about the crash. I wasn't sure if the prosecutors wanted to use it. When we arrived, I was told they didn't. I wish they would have as it was powerful, although it would have been hard for me. I haven't listened to it since the day of the crash.

At the courthouse, we went down to the victim's impact room and met Steve's brother and other Davis family members. I wore my new angel wing necklace so Abby could give me strength. I had printed out my statement to read to help me get through it. I spoke to Steve's brother and his wife and Terri's mom. The victim's advocate came in and said to go upstairs because all of your hometown is here. The hearing was in a small courtroom with standing room only. The press was there, and while we were waiting, I asked the cameraman not to use the photos of Lexi in the hospital that I would show. I didn't want them public.

I had created a PowerPoint of photos and videos that was too large to email, so I gave the prosecutors the thumb drive when we came to court. Court finally started about 10:30 a.m. We were told the delay was because the judge was reading the victim-impact statements. Some in the courtroom were wearing t-shirts with Abby's picture on them and some wore "Lexi" buttons. Someone from the prosecutor's office passed out tissues to the crowd; I guess they knew how emotional it would be.

Finally, the prosecutors told me the PowerPoint was fine and Liz, the witness, would go first; then me, Ray, the Davis family. To prepare them, I had warned Steve and Terri that I had photos of the girls together.

Liz, the witness, was the first to testify. She talked about how the driver had been swerving for about two miles. She was scared, so she had her daughter pass him, saying, "We need to get away from that truck." They were in front of the accident when it happened. When she heard the crash, she had her daughter pull over and she ran to the scene. She saw the truck driver first, and he said he was fine, so she went to Abby's car. She couldn't open the door, so she went to the passenger side. She talked about how Abby didn't have a pulse, and Lexi's was weak. She also said Lexi's breathing was shallow, what she called brain-stem breathing which meant the person may soon die. I was sobbing. She talked about the effect this has had on her, as well as her daughter, causing her to need trauma counseling.

I was the next to go. I walked behind the prosecutor's table so I wouldn't go near the driver. I turned my chair facing the judge. I didn't want to see the driver, and the judge was my audience—the one I had to convince. At one point, the defense attorney interrupted me and said my testimony wasn't relevant. He was overruled. When I was talking about Lexi's vision loss, the judge informed me that Lexi had explained that in her statement. I said I hadn't read her statement. He also asked me if we had health insurance. I told him we had four different policies. Usually when I tell someone that, I will say Ray and I got married so there would be ample insurance coverage. For some reason, I think because I would have broken down, I didn't tell the judge. I hadn't been able to say anything publicly due to the legal issues, so this was my first chance to talk about how horrible our journey had been. I talked a lot about Abby and how the girls were side by side in all the photos from Europe and how they stayed side by side until Abby was *killed!* I showed videos of Lexi re-learning to swallow, eat, and walk and how, when she should have been graduating high school, I was standing outside her room as the nurses changed her diaper. When I was talking about my fears for Lexi's future, I talked about self-medicating, and how the risk of suicide is much greater in TBI patients. The defense attorney objected. He said I was straying, and the prosecutors stood up and said, "This is what she fears." He was overruled. I completed my presentation without breaking down. My voice cracked a few times. I tend to talk fast when I am nervous, so I had written "slow" on all the pages. I had also highlighted areas where I wanted to pause to let the words and emotions sink in.

After I finished, it was Ray's turn. He kissed me when we passed on his way up. He was emotional, and it took him a few minutes to compose himself. They had left the last photo up that I had of Lexi and Abby in my Power-Point. They had him identify the two girls. He finally was able to get out what he wanted to say. His testimony was short, but to the point: The driver had a choice, and he chose to do drugs and drink, and then drive a fully loaded delivery truck.

After we were done, Abby's two aunts spoke, and you could hear everyone crying. It was hard to hear how her death affected many people. I was bawling. Good thing we had the tissues.

Abby's grandma spoke. I was sitting right behind her husband who was crying; I was crying; everyone was crying. Then Abby's brother spoke. He had a hard time getting started. He looked so grown up in his suit and bow tie. He was 16, and he talked about how he and Abby fought 75 percent of the time, but that made the other 25 percent that much sweeter. He talked about how the morning of the crash he was ready for school, but he found Abby asleep. She told him that someone else needed to drive him because she was going to the beach. If you had a heart, it was broken listening to him.

The defense attorney kept objecting to various things that we said. The prosecutors explained this was how the person's life was affected by this tragedy. The defense attorney also objected to some of the victims' impact statements that had asked for a harsh sentence. The judge explained he had been on the bench for 21 years and he knew how to exclude what wasn't relative to his decision-making process. The people writing these letters are not legal experts, and he can mentally set aside what isn't allowed by law.

Last were Abby's parents. They both talked about the

day of the accident. I didn't realize someone else told Steve about the accident. I knew he had gone to the scene, because he had called me from there. Listening to Steve and Terri's grief was certainly another level of this misery. I think listening must have been like being at Abby's funeral, but the emotions were magnified by how this tragedy has affected everyone for 16 months.

Terri's testimony ended with a video. The defense tried to get it excluded. Abby's cousin, whose Mom I sat next to, had created a video of Abby as a school project and to help him deal with his grief. I was crying so hard, especially when they had photos of Abby and Lexi. At one point there was a photo of Abby's CRV. I had never seen the car, and when I did, I said, "Oh God," and buried my head in Ray's shoulder. I caught only a glimpse, but it was too much. I had talked that morning to Steve's brother about how I hadn't seen the car, and he said that was good.

Before Terri spoke, we had taken a 10-minute break, and I explained to the public relations liaison for the court that I couldn't listen to the driver's family talk about how great he was, and we were going to leave during that part of the proceedings. I had been planning this all along. It was about 1:30 p.m. She told me the judge might call for a lunch break. I listened to Terri and watched the video and then left, passing his family. His family had left the courtroom for at least the video. Ray stayed for a few minutes and then left. Apparently, his supporters were saying he grew up in the projects and started drinking early, blah blah . . .

Ray and I went to lunch and kept checking our phones. We were pulling into a parking spot at the courthouse when I received the text that he was given the *maximum sentence of 47 years*. I screamed and started to cry. I took a few minutes to compose myself as his family was leaving and were parked near us, so we waited until they were gone to get out of our car.

We had been told to expect about a 20-to-30-year sentence and we had steeled ourselves for a shorter one. Very rarely do drunk drivers get the maximum sentence, but he did. The judge said it was one of the worst cases of drunk driving he had seen and that the driver had a choice in what he did that day.

When we walked up to the courthouse, supporters hugged us. I told the press I would talk to them, but I wanted to find the prosecutors first. We finally found everyone in a small conference room. First, I hugged the prosecutors and the police officers. The police officers were there even though they weren't testifying. I was touched by their presence. Then we hugged the Davises. We briefly discussed that he may appeal, but the prosecutors weren't overly concerned. A million years will not bring Abby back or make Lexi whole again, but I was so happy he was given the maximum sentence.

I was also glad this part of the legal drama was over. I had been dreading it for a long time. A part of me felt like a weight had been lifted off my shoulders and another part had so much fresh heartbreak that I could barely breathe.

I spoke briefly to the media, something I hadn't been able to do because of all the legal issues. Because we had a category-4 hurricane heading toward us that day, we were bumped to the second story on the news, although I did get a notification on my phone about the sentencing, meaning it was still a major news story.

When we reached the car where we had left our phones, mine was blowing up with texts and phone calls. I posted the sentencing results on Facebook. With a major hurricane barreling down on us, we stopped at three stores trying to find water. I said to Ray, "I wish we could have had a few days of peace before a hurricane arrives."

NOTE: See Appendix for our victim-impact statements.

Chapter 21

Abby: In Memoriam

"Your wings may have been ready, but my heart wasn't . . ."
– Anonymous

Why, oh why? This book wouldn't be complete without a chapter on Abby Elizabeth Davis. Abby was incredibly beautiful both inside and outside. Abby was in my Girl Scout Daisy troop when the girls were in kindergarten. I remember her as a sweet, polite girl who did Irish dancing. Abby was also in the group of girls who went to 4-H camp with Lexi. Lexi and Abby became very close once they went to Europe together in high school.

I got to know Abby better as she and Lexi were always together in 11th and 12th grade. I remember Abby sitting at my counter eating pancakes with no makeup on after a sleepover. When Lexi's date asked her to senior prom he brought her coffee and flowers. I thought that was so cute. Lexi told me Abby had suggested the coffee.

When we went to Hokie weekend for students accepted at Virginia Tech in April of 2017. Abby and her family were there. While we were there, Lexi decided to commit to Virginia Tech. Abby's family was traveling on to North Carolina, and because Abby wanted to stay longer, I told her she could come home with us. The three of us

spent that morning at the bookstore as both girls had made their decisions and wanted to buy lots of Tech clothes. We also took a bunch of photos around the campus. On our way home, we stopped at the Natural Bridge, a beautiful formation that is a state park. We spent a few hours there enjoying ourselves. We then left and went on to Charlottesville to spend the night. It turned out that Lexi's friend Sarah was in town as she had chosen the University of Virginia. After dinner, I dropped off the girls to hang out with Sarah, and her mom and I had a drink. Lexi and Abby walked around UVA dressed head to toe in Tech gear, not caring that the schools are rivals. I later learned that Lexi and Abby had been a huge comfort to Sarah, who had recently found out that her boyfriend of three years had been cheating on her. They cheered her up, talking about plans and all the fun they'd have in college. I have been so touched by the stories of Abby's kindness—to the underappreciated and the underdogs. She would have made a huge difference in the world.

On the way home the next day, I had told both girls their future was so bright they needed sunglasses.

Chapter 22

The Dragonfly Story

"Legend has it that dragonflies were given an extra set of wings so that angels could ride on their back, smaller than small. Yet whenever you see a winged masterpiece, you can be certain that an angel has come down from heaven to visit you."

– Heather Fitzpatrick

The last week I was in Atlanta, I received a text from Emma's mom saying she had a friend, Laura, who was home during the day and wanted to help with Lexi's care. In her text she said, "She wants to help with anything." I texted her back that I thought I had already found someone for the caregiving role, but told her I would call Laura. I was too busy getting everything ready to leave Atlanta for me to call her right away. We had to pack up the car and clean the apartment. It wasn't until I was at the Atlanta airport that I had time to call her. When I left Ray and Lexi, as well as the apartment for the last time, I was emotional. I had said goodbye to the friends we had met and the amazing counselors and therapists. I shed quite a few tears thinking about how far we had come, but I was afraid of what was to come at home. In Atlanta, as hard as it was, we had been in a sort of a bubble. We were closing one chapter, but getting ready for a new one.

Once I was at the gate waiting for my flight, I called Laura. She told me the most fantastic story—even today I get goosebumps and am haunted by it. I asked her to send me an email with the story so I would get it correct.

Here is her story:

> As I was sitting on my back patio, I noticed two dragonflies on my railing. One was the prettiest blue/green color I've ever seen. *She* was glowing. They were sitting there like they were talking to each other when the other one flew away but came right back. The bluish one sat very quiet, and then kind of nudged, I swear "kissed," the other one towards the pond, and she flew away. As soon as it flew out of site, I saw the medical helicopter flying overhead. I didn't understand but I started to cry. The whole time the dragonfly was watching me, and then she flew right at me. It was a moment in time that I will never forget.

It turns out Laura lives on a pond that is close to the crash site. (The photo used for the cover of this book is of that pond.) She didn't know about the crash, but when she saw the news that evening, she called a friend and told her about what she had seen.

After our phone conversation ended, I was in the airport crying my eyes out. *Abby sent Lexi back to us.* I was so emotional and upset that the poor guy I sat next to on the airplane heard my entire story. Usually I was reluctant to tell people about our story, but now it all came pouring out. He was super nice, and even sent me an email the next day saying how moved he was.

Before I heard Laura's story, Abby's friends and family were posting on Facebook about seeing dragonflies near them. The dragonflies would show up at key times, such as when Abby's brother was having surgery. When her dad walked outside for a few minutes, a dragonfly was waiting for him. I saw my first dragonfly one evening shortly after the crash as I was leaving the ICU and walking to my car. The first Sunday I was home from Atlanta I saw a beautiful tiffany-blue dragonfly sitting on a bush near my car. In the Native American culture, the dragonfly represents a spirit that has passed on.

I had always felt that Abby was watching over Lexi, now I felt I had proof. Every time I see a dragonfly now, I pause to thank her for being here, and for watching over all of us.

Chapter 23

Puppy Love

*"When I needed a hand, I reached
down and found your paw."*

– Unknown

Our 13-year-old dog, Cloe, had died the end of March 2017. She had been sick since early January, but had rebounded. When she passed, it was the hardest thing I had to tell Lexi—until we had to tell her about Abby.

Although I missed coming home to Cloe, it was great having a clean house. No way we could have taken care of a pet in addition to everything else.

Once the crash happened, and especially because Lexi had been petting Abby's puppy as it happened, I knew she needed a dog.

I wanted to wait to get another dog until she had been home for a while, allowing Lexi to settle in first. I didn't want to spend a ton of money either. Even before the crash she was asking for a dog and she wanted a Pomski. I was pushing for a rescue dog, but for some reason Lexi didn't want that. Her caregiver found a miniature golden retriever online. I spoke to the breeder and explained the situation. The breeder had a puppy that had been returned to her as the couple decided to break up right after they brought the dog home. Her daughter had felt sorry for the dog, so the dog had been sleeping with her. She told me the dog loved to cuddle, and she thought he would be perfect. She also had other puppies to choose from just in case. At the end of October, I left work early, and Marshall, Lexi, and I drove out to see the puppy. It was a four-hour drive one way to see the dog. The breeder lived on a farm and had the four male puppies in a room. Our dog came right up to Lexi. The other dogs didn't warm up to her until about 10 minutes later. Although I wanted a female dog, the breeder had told me that the males were more loving, so she had only the males out. On the ride home, Lexi was trying to come up with a name. One of the names she came up with was Davis. I really didn't want her to name the puppy Davis. It would be too hard on all of us and a constant reminder of Abby. The dog was supposed to help her heal. By the time we arrived home over five hours later, she had decided on Harley.

We all fell in love with Harley, but Lexi is obsessed with him. When she is home, she wants to be with him. When she goes back to school, she cries for at least a half hour. When she is at school, she calls to check on him. She likes to see him, so she prefers to Facetime. I love that because I get to actually see her. She is always worrying about his eating and us taking him for walks. She drives us nuts. It is hard having a puppy again, but I know how important he is for Lexi.

Almost eighteen months after the crash, I came downstairs on a Saturday morning and turned on the TV to watch the news like I do every morning, and a story about the crash was on TV. I stood there with tears rolling down my cheeks, and Harley came up to me to console me. Yes, he is good *for all of us.*

Chapter 24

The People You Meet Along the Way

"Strength doesn't come from what you can do. It comes from overcoming the things you once thought you couldn't."
– Rikki Rogers

Once something like this happens, it is fascinating the web of connections you have with others who've had a similar experience. Many, many people reached out to us whose loved one has a TBI, spinal cord injury, or another traumatic experience. They were all such a huge help. These connections are part of the reason I wanted to write this book. Because a lot of people helped us, I want to be able to help others.

Social media is a fantastic way to reach out to others. Post if you can what you are going through, and you will be amazed at who you will hear from. It's how I received lots of leads on apartments in Atlanta. Many people reached out to us, wanting to help. Virginia Tech is a large university in Virginia and I was part of the Virginia Tech Parents Facebook page. I received a lot of love from the Hokie family because Lexi had committed to Virginia Tech. It was truly unbelievable.

I have become a TBI resource and have reached out to other families or have had friends refer people to me. I am happy to pay it back with the all the help we received.

When we arrived at Shepherd Center, we bonded with families whose child had a TBI or a stroke, including quite a few 17-to-24-year-olds who had had strokes. I encourage you to exchange cell phone numbers or email address; it is a great network to have for therapy referrals, or supplements. We now have a Facebook group with the people we met to share our kids' triumphs. No one else can imagine what you are going through; these people can.

We have also kept in touch with various people who helped with Lexi's medical care. One of the flight paramedics had experienced a similar tragedy in his own life, and the day of Lexi's crash was his first day back to work. His family member also went to Shepherd Center. There was also a young woman who was doing her first rounds as a resident physician's assistant. Because I was almost always there for rounds, I observed her not only with Lexi but also as she asked questions of the doctors. She reminded me a lot of Lexi, and one day I told her that. When we were leaving for Atlanta, she gave me her email address, and we have stayed in touch. We are also in touch with some of the nurses as well as the doctor who did her arm surgery. These are people I think will be a part of our lives forever.

As I have mentioned, Lexi wanted to be a doctor before the crash, and still does. She is going to shadow her orthopedic surgeon this winter. Lots of people will give her recommendations for medical school due to all the care she's received. Lexi has joked that she didn't have a tragic story to write about when she was writing her essays for undergrad. Now she has a whopper of a tragedy to write about for medical school.

Soon after Lexi was back home from Atlanta, we visited the burn trauma ICU and the staff there. She was hesitant about going back, but I insisted. Ray, Marshall, and I took her. When we had left the hospital initially, they had asked us to come back once we returned—this was how they were able to tell us about the Shepherd Center's miracles. It was important to me to be able to have her walk back into the ICU. It was obvious how much it meant to them to see her, bringing many to tears. All of them were amazed at how far she had come. More than one nurse told me this is why they work so hard—to see the miracles that come back. One of the nurses said to me, "I wouldn't have recognized you." I said, "Yes, it is amazing what makeup and sleep does for a person." I will always be forever grateful to the entire medical team that helped in Lexi's recovery.

Chapter 25

Our Community's Overwhelming Support and Love

"You raise me up to more than I can be."
– Roman Tyan, lyrics from "You Raise Me Up"

The Saturday before the crash, Ray and I said how fortunate we were to have such wonderful friends in our lives. We didn't know how that would be put to the test. From the beginning, our friends were extraordinary, including running errands for us, bringing coffee or meals to the hospital.

We received notes and cards from Lexi's friends, teachers, places where she had volunteered, from Hokies and graduates of her high school going back decades, and even total strangers with no connection to us. My friend Nancy who owns a barbershop had a huge card in her shop that her customers signed. At school they had a table for the girls' classmates to write notes. I have saved all of them in two large boxes. I have always known how special Lexi is, but I was moved to see how she had touched many people's lives.

Signs were all over town from their high school, to the

YMCA, to local restaurants, showing love and support for both families. I didn't see many of them, but friends sent me photos. We also had a few strangers make us beautiful prayer shawls and quilts I will treasure forever.

My friend Kristen, who started the crowdsourcing page, was the contact person. It turned into a part-time job with people asking how they could help or how to get the money they had raised to us. The online donation page made such a huge difference. When we were approved for Shepherd Center, the social worker at the hospital told us sometimes insurance won't cover the medical flight. I told her it was fine; we had raised over $10,000 in 24 hours. We were able to give Lexi so many extras, including the expensive burgers she craved in Atlanta when she wouldn't eat the hospital food, and more important, alternative treatments that weren't covered by insurance. I will be forever grateful to everyone who donated any amount, large or small. It was overwhelming all the love we received from all over the world.

We received so many acts of kindness. Many companies were fundraising for the girls: an auto repair shop that I had never been to, and a burrito restaurant, pizza place, jewelry companies and kitchen supply companies, to name a few. People who had never met either family were touched and wanted to help. Right after the crash two women who we didn't know made and sold over 1,000 t-shirts. The shirts were shipped to people as far away as Washington State, North Carolina, Texas, Massachusetts, Maine, New Hampshire, and Georgia. That was very special. When I see people wearing the shirts, it warms my heart.

Once we were home, the high school baseball team had a fundraiser called "Costumes for a Cause" and they selected Lexi to be their cause. Unfortunately, she had her fourth surgery right before the event and couldn't go. I am glad she didn't go because it would have been too many people and too much noise, both of which were hard for her to deal with. Normally not that many people attend baseball games at the high school, but that night hundreds of people were there, in fact, they pre-sold over 600 tickets. A local major league baseball player who lives in the area was there. I had my photo taken with him and he was a total sweetheart. Ray stayed home to take care of Lexi, so I sent him a photo as he is a huge baseball fan. There were silent auction items and food for sale. All proceeds went to Lexi. I said a few short words and almost made it through without crying.

I heard Sheryl Sandberg interviewed about her book, *Option B.* before the crash. She said to be specific with what you will do when a tragedy strikes a friend; not "I will bring you a meal," but, "I am bringing you a hamburger, what don't you like on your hamburger"? This stuck with me when I initially heard it. I tried to take that to heart when we needed help, and now, I try to pay it forward with others. Choose something and do it: laundry, errands, meals, etc. When someone is going through a tragedy, they need help with every little thing. Many people are too overwhelmed to even know what they need, so just do it.

The social worker at Shepherd Center told Ray a tragedy of this magnitude could wipe out a family financially. We appreciated every dollar we received.

Our goal was to get Lexi back to as close to 100 percent as possible, and *that takes money.*

Chapter 26

Out-of-the-Box Therapies

"Innovation happens because there are people out there doing and trying a lot of different things."
– Edward Felten

I took ideas and suggestions from all kinds of places. Doctors and friends suggested some therapies as well as some recommendations on various Facebook TBI pages. I have been willing to try anything that might help if I don't think it will cause harm.

One of the biggest problems Lexi has is her vision loss. I have tried everything I can to improve her vision.

Our eye specialist recommended neurovision. It is a computer program where you click on dots. It has been proven to be helpful. It was expensive, but Lexi told me she would use it. Unfortunately, she ended up hating the program as she thought it was boring. We constantly fought over this because I desperately wanted her to have as much vision as possible. Because she can't drive, if she wants to go anywhere, she expects us to drop everything and run her there. I would beg her to at least complete the program to try to get enough vision back in order to drive. She promised me she would, but she didn't. I had access to a report on the web site so I could see when she did it.

It was a total waste of money for us but if you can, I would recommend trying it as it has helped others.

We had her in vision therapy both in Atlanta and at home. When we were in Atlanta, she was much better about doing the homework because there were no distractions. Once we returned home, she didn't do it in the same consistent fashion. Again, we fought over this too. Her vision for up-close work did improve somewhat; her eyes were able to work together better, which is important for schoolwork.

My counselor told me about hyperbaric chamber treatments. She was reviewing the test results from before and after the treatments. She thought it might help Lexi. The treatment is a series of 40 sessions where you are in a tube that looks like a propane tank. Up to four people can be in the tube at once. The patients put on scrubs and enter the chamber; they then have a hood put on their head and hook up tubes so oxygen enters the hood. They are breathing a high amount of oxygen. I was worried that Lexi might get claustrophobic, but we decided to try it. Someone went in with Lexi for the first few times. Ideally, you want to do 40 treatments without a break. Before the first session Lexi took a cognitive test that established her starting point. For the first few sessions, she took an herbal supplement to help her relax. I was there for the first session, but after that I was there only on my days off. Unfortunately, Lexi got a cold and also had surgery, so she couldn't do 40 days with as much consistency as I would have liked. It was hard for me to see improvement being with her every day. When she was tested at the end, her scores significantly improved by 20 percent. Her thinking was faster, she was able to put words together, and her memory was improved. Lexi saw an improvement. Hyperbaric Oxygen Therapy is considered investigational; thus, it is not covered by health insurance. We were blessed in that we had the crowdsourcing donations to pay for it.

We tried float therapy, which helped her to sleep. You are in a pod-type large bathtub with very salty water and you lie there for 60 minutes. I find it boring, but she thought it helped her to relax and improved her sleep. She did that a few times.

When we were in Atlanta, I found a wonderful masseuse. I took Lexi to him a few times, and he especially worked her left shoulder. She felt that helped her.

Once we were home, she continued having significant trouble sleeping, a very common occurrence in brain injury patients. Her rehab doctor suggested she have a sleep study to rule out breathing issues and sleep apnea. In November we drove her to the sleep study center and left her for the night. She had to get up early, which she hated, but we took her to get some breakfast afterwards, and then she was able to come home and go back to sleep. Her results were fine. Her difficulty sleeping goes on, and melatonin hasn't helped. The only thing that has helped to sleep is the supplement bioZzz.

Yoga and meditation have been proven to be helpful for brain injury patients. She did yoga before the crash, but because of her arm, she won't go to a class or even have someone come to the house to do yoga.

We both tried biofeedback sessions, which she felt helped her focus. I didn't see any benefit. Of course, it wasn't covered by insurance. I mentioned it to my counselor, and she told me about a device she uses called Muse, which can be purchased online. It is a band that you wear on your head. There is an app for a smart phone that you download that plays sounds and gives you feedback. If your mind is wandering, it sounds like a storm. The goal is to calm your mind and hear the birds. It costs about $250, but I was paying $150 for each biofeedback session, so for me it was worth it. Anyone can use it but needs the app on their phone. I use it all the time as it helps with my anxiety.

Exercise is important for anyone's brain, but especially for someone with a TBI. Lexi worked out before the crash—that is why she could do hundreds of sit-ups once she was no longer unconscious. Now that she is at Virginia Tech, she gets up early to go work out. This is good for her brain and helps her deal with stress.

Cognitive FX, Provo, Utah

A friend told me about Cognitive FX treatment center located in Utah. She took her son there after he had suffered multiple concussions in his teens. It helped him greatly to feel better and think clearly. I immediately checked it out and called to make an appointment. Cognitive FX is primarily a place for people who have had concussions. When I talked to the doctor, she asked me how long Lexi had been unconscious. When I told her two weeks, she didn't think they could help her. She was expecting two to 10 minutes at most. I explained that Lexi had been at Shepherd Center and was currently in college taking two classes. We set up a time for all three of us to talk. After talking to Lexi, she felt she could help her. We were skeptical, but I thought it was worth a try.

I am from Utah originally, and hadn't been home in about five years. We set up the therapy for the week after Lexi would be finished with her classes. Ray, Lexi, and I flew to Salt Lake City the weekend before therapy would begin. I have a lot of friends in Salt Lake City, so it was fun to introduce Ray to them as well as for them to see Lexi. Happily, we had time to spend with my family.

Monday morning, we drove to Provo, Utah to start her week of therapy. Cognitive FX starts with a functional MRI. They ask you questions during an MRI to determine how blood is flowing in your brain. I brought her medical records and the MRI from the ICU. That afternoon they showed us the results of her functional MRI. They were testing for 14 different things. We thought her results were good, considering the severity of her injury. The doctor told us that she was really struggling. Ray and I were both shocked that her learning was ranked so low. They asked her if it was hard for her to learn, and she said, "Yes." Because she had earned A's, we didn't realize it was so hard for her to be in school.

The week Lexi was there, it was all women patients. I ran errands and did other things while she was in therapy, so I didn't connect with most of the other people there, except for one woman from Florida. She had been snowboarding at Park City, Utah, the previous winter with a helmet, but fell and hit her head. She has three young children and couldn't function. She had undergone other therapies and this was her last resort. Ironically her husband is a doctor. She connected with Lexi and me, and as a mom she understood what I was going through.

The program is one week, Monday to Friday. That Friday morning as we were getting ready, Lexi told me she could put her pants on her left leg without holding on to something. Her brain injury was to her right side, so it was her left side that was affected. *This progress was huge.*

That same morning, I asked the Florida woman how she was doing, and she said it was the first morning in 10 months she woke up without a headache. I was amazed.

After a few therapies on Friday, the participants had another functional MRI. I was on pins and needles waiting for the results. Lexi had felt they helped her greatly. She had even asked some of the therapists why these treatments weren't being done at other places. She felt she had improved dramatically in that week. When we saw the results, we were shocked. She was now normal in almost all tests, and the lines were touching, showing her brain was working much better; before they were all over the place. This means the blood was flowing to all parts of her brain. She was not back to where she was before the crash, but Lexi had made great strides in a short time.

Cognitive FX's treatment may not be for everyone. It is expensive, and right now, insurance doesn't cover it. They do have scholarships available. They are looking at opening a center in Atlanta soon, in conjunction with a sports medicine center. I highly recommend checking it out.

We also tried many vitamins and supplements. At one-point Lexi was taking about 10 different vitamins, including various vitamin Bs, melatonin, CQ10, and an optic nerve formula supplement. I have spent hundreds of dollars on vitamins, and many remain in my cabinet. Now she is at school, she doesn't want to be taking that many pills, but she takes a multi-vitamin in addition to her prescribed pills. Be sure to tell the doctors what you are taking so there are no adverse effects.

Chapter 27

The Personal Rollercoaster of Grief

"Don't cry because it's over.
Smile because it happened."

– Dr. Seuss

I have learned much from this tragedy, but one thing that stands out *is how people grieve.* Grief is a complex emotion and everyone grieves differently. There is no right or wrong way to process sadness and grief. I am incredibly grateful that Lexi is with us, and doing as well as she is, but our lives will never be the same. In the beginning I would cry over prom and graduation, and Ray would say to me, "She's here, that is what matters." He didn't get that I was grieving for what we lost: prom, graduation, her lifeguard job, her graduation trip, our trip to see Neil Diamond, and so many other things. When I spoke to my counselor about the losses, she explained that it is okay for me to grieve what was stolen from us, because that is natural and normal. I needed to hear that.

I have often wondered how I would feel about Abby's death if Lexi hadn't been with her. I have no doubt I would have been profoundly affected, but I am quite sure it is exponentially worse because Lexi was also a victim. I can't imagine how I would feel if this was "just" an accident and no drugs and or alcohol was involved. It makes it much harder, this was all preventable.

A few months before the crash I was at a friend's house to help with prep work for the after-prom event. The Davises attended and I remember thinking how we would be linked because the girls were going to Tech together. Now no matter what, we will always be linked by this tragedy. I clearly remember telling them the Sunday after the crash, "We are on different paths, but both are extraordinarily difficult."

About eight months after the crash, I was talking to an acquaintance who said, "Lexi needs to get over this." I don't think I responded. *This is not something any of us can "get over."* This was a major trauma in all our lives. We are all dealing with it in our own way, and I am sure with time it will fade a bit, but at least for me, I will never "get over" it. I will always grieve the loss of Abby as well as what we lost.

It took me over a year to finally give in and sell Lexi's car. Her vision hasn't improved so she can't drive. It was emotional to accept the fact she wouldn't be able to use the car. She was excited when she received her license and had driven for almost exactly two years. I am working on trying to get her a self-driving car as soon as they are available. Driving is freedom, which is important to everyone, especially a young woman with her life ahead of her.

Lexi sent me information about a study-abroad program, but one of the requirements is being a strong swimmer. Before the crash, she was a great swimmer, a lifeguard and on a swim team. Now her arm doesn't move, so she can't swim. A study-abroad option has been taken away from her. I have no doubt that as we all live our daily lives, we will have constant, unexpected moments of grief.

Chapter 28

Moving Forward

*"As for accomplishments, I just did what
I had to do as things came along."*
– Eleanor Roosevelt

How I wish I didn't have this story to tell. Writing this book was like going back in time. I would tell Ray I was going down the rabbit hole when I sat at the computer to write. Time would stop and I would relive both the good and the bad.

My life is divided into *before the crash and after*. I hope as time goes on that line will become less apparent. I continue to grieve for everything we have lost, both the large and small, and live with many things that affect my daily life. Even after all this time, I am a wreck when I am driving, and I'm even worse as a passenger. I scare Ray when he is driving as I jump and yell at any possible danger. I am trying to control my fear, but it is difficult. I hope this gets better with time. I haven't been to the restaurant where Abby worked because I can't face it. My life has changed in immeasurable ways.

It is very hard for me to have Lexi so far away. I begged her to go to college closer to home, but she wouldn't hear of it. When she first was back home, a nurse from the insurance company came over and asked me how I allowed her to leave the house. She is a mom, so she gets how hard it is for me to let her live her life. If I could wrap her in bubble wrap, I would. Ultimately, I know in my heart I have done everything I can for her, and she must be allowed to live her life.

With Lexi away at school, our relationship has improved. Part of it is she continues to heal and mature; part of it is that she is hundreds of miles away. I saw posts at the beginning of the semester from parents who hadn't heard from their students for two weeks. Not me. She calls me at least once a day, and we exchange multiple texts and emails. The other night she called me after having attended a meeting about study-abroad programs. She said, "I am so grateful for the relationship we have." She told me I had raised her to love travel and to be independent and go off and do what she wanted. I was very happy. As Ray says, "The older they get, the smarter we get."

The crash comes up in her life in so many ways, not only her limitations, but other reminders. Three months into fall semester, she was at a football game, and the young woman who was going to be Abby's roommate came up and introduced herself to Lexi. It made me happy that they connected, but also sad that Abby was not there with them. Lexi told me she likes being at school better than she likes being at home. At home she is occasionally recognized, where at school fewer people recognized her for being the victim of a horrific car crash. Lexi does not want to be defined by this event.

I am the type of person who acts when something bad happens because it gives me some feeling of control. When my dad died, I wrote the obituary and planned the funeral. With this, I could barely get through every day and my only focus was to get Lexi the best care I could. Now that she is in school, I have been able to focus on trying to help others.

Hosting a Support Group

Once the legal issues were resolved, I was able to start hosting my support group. I have now held multiple meetings and twelve families attend. I received a text from one of my members apologizing she was too tired to come. I responded with, "You never need to apologize to me, I get it." That is one of the most important things about a support group. No one else can understand this journey, but they can. At the second meeting two young men exchanged phone numbers so they could play games together. This is what I want to come out of the support group—connections and friendships. Lexi called me when I was walking into my latest support group. I told her where I was, and it needed to be quick. After we hung up, she sent me this text: "I'm so proud of you mom and all the work you are putting into helping people with brain injuries. It is so amazing, and I know people are so grateful for it (:"

That is all the thanks I need.

I am also now able to get more involved with Mothers Against Drunk Driving and the Brain Injury Association. Both organizations will receive proceeds from this book. I am working with the local courts to speak to young people as they get their driver's license. Although I will never know if I save one life, I hope if a new driver thinks back to my talk, he or she might not drink and drive or might even take the keys away from an impaired driver.

19 Months (or 579 Days) Since the Crash

As I write this, Lexi is now home and has finished her first full semester at Virginia Tech. She did remarkably well. When people ask me how she is doing, the only thing I can say is *she is a miracle.* She loves being at school. She complains how the area we live in is awful for someone who can't drive, and she is correct. When we chose this house, we didn't think we would need public transportation. She gets frustrated depending on us to get her everywhere. She doesn't want to ask her friends to drive her places. I told her that if things were reversed, she would drive her friend around, but she *does not* like to ask for help. When she graduates, she plans to live in a city with good public transportation.

Grief washes over me on a regular basis. Earlier this month, we attended a Mothers Against Drunk Driving candlelight vigil. I also get phone calls and mail from the Department of Corrections regarding where the offender will be housed; and it was recently Abby's 20th birthday, so that was a painful day. How I wish I could go back in time to 580 days ago. But I know I couldn't have stopped Lexi from going to the beach. Even if I told her that Abby would die, and she would be severely injured, she would have told me I was being ridiculous.

A few weeks ago, I spoke to another mom whose child was at Shepherd Center with us. She had contacted me to ask what therapies Lexi had found helpful. She told me when Lexi first arrived at Shepherd and they were in the gym together. Lexi had grabbed her arm, told her she needed help, and asked her to call her mom. Learning this was like a punch to my gut! We were there, so I was probably talking to the doctor or had run to the bathroom. It killed me to hear this even so many months later.

As hard as this has been sharing our successes and setbacks, if I have helped one person it is worth it. I believe in my heart that Lexi survived for a reason.

Our story continues. Lexi is a miracle; however, I know she has a lifetime of challenges ahead of her that she wouldn't have had without the crash. I hope and pray Lexi makes ongoing progress and lives a long and happy life. She has never been shy, yet she does not want attention that comes from the crash. I trust, though, she will eventually find a balance with her emotions about all that has happened. She is focused now on becoming a doctor, and I have no doubt, especially with what she has been through, that she will be an excellent one. If she decides to do something else, that is fine too. She is driven to succeed, and despite everything she has been through, she is an inspiration to many, especially me. I have always been honored to be her mom. In fact, "Mom" has always been my favorite title.

Acknowledgments

Lexi would never have survived without the immediate help she received from the people who were first on the scene. To the first responders, the flight crew on the helicopter, the emergency room staff, and all the nurses and doctors in the Burn Trauma ICU, we will be forever grateful.

Lexi also wouldn't be doing as well as she is without the outstanding staff at Shepherd Center in Atlanta. Special thanks to everyone there. Miracles happen at Shepherds, and our daughter is living proof.

To our children, Marshall, Vern, Ellie, and her husband, David, thank you. You all stepped up and were amazing. A special thanks to my new sister-in-law, Olga, as well as my best friend, Jamie. They both flew in from California when we needed them.

Thank you also to all our friends, family, Lexi's teachers, employers and people who she had touched in her life, as well as total strangers who donated or planned fundraisers. To all the strangers who had walked this road of traumatic brain injury before me and reached out to help me, I am so grateful, and I am trying to pay it forward. To everyone all over the world who prayed for her, the prayers were answered. No words can ever express our gratitude.

And most important, to my incredible husband, Ray: I love you. No one else in the universe would have willingly stepped into this nightmare and married me, but you did. You are my rock, and I couldn't have survived this without you.

Many people helped make this book a reality. It couldn't have gotten done without the support and encouragement of my awesome husband, Ray, who was my shoulder to cry on when I was writing it and who shed tears each time he has read it. Others who were invaluable: Sandra, Debbie and Ginni, Lori, Kristen and Carolyn for giving me feedback on my writing. Connie, my editor (www.WordsandDeedsInc.com) and Ann at Fuzion Print (www.FuzionPrint.com) for helping me get it printed.

Resources

Be cautious when you do research about traumatic brain injury outcomes because every brain injury is different.

Websites:

The sites below I found to be helpful and have good information to help both the patient and the caregivers in your journey:

- www.biausa.org – Brain Injury Association of America. Also check for your state/local chapters

- www.braininjurynetwork.org – for survivors and families

- www.brainline.org

- www.cdc.gov/traumaticbraininjury/outcomes.html

- www.brainandspinalcord.org

- www.dana.org

- www.neuroskills.com – monthly summary of worldwide research

- www.loveyourbrain.com – a great site plus has lots of yoga info for TBI survivors

- www.youcantimaginebook.com – the website for this book

Apps for a Smartphone:

- BrainHQ

- 10% Happier

- Power of Positive Thinking
- Calm

Facebook:

Some of the Facebook pages I found helpful:

- Amy's TBI tribe
- TBI Survivors and Caregivers
- Traumatic Brain Injury Healing and Recovery Support Group
- TBI Mothers
- Life After Brain Injury: The Personal Side of Traumatic Brain Injury
- Traumatic Brain Injury Healthy Alternatives
- Traumatic or Acquired Brain Injury Support Group
- Mallory's Movement Against Drunk Driving
- NSUnturned
- optionB.org

Books:

I didn't have the time or energy to read many books, but here are a few I found helpful:

Goldstein, Joel. *No Stone Unturned: A Father's Memoir of His Son's Encounter with Traumatic Brain Injury.* Washington, DC: Potomac Books 2012

Sandberg, Sheryl and Grant, Adam. *Option B*, New York: Alfred A. Knoff 2017

Neal, Mary, M.D. *To Heaven and Back: A Doctor's Extraordinary Account of Her Death, Heaven, Angels, and Life Again: A True Story*

Zellmer, Amy. *Life with a Traumatic Brain Injury*. Fuzion Print 2015

Woodruff, Lee and Bob. *In An Instant: A Families Journey of Love and Healing*, New York: Random House, 2007

Grant, Sarah and David. *To Be Inspired: Stories of Courage and Hope after Brain Injury*, 2016

Other tips:

You can order a Brain Injury ID card that you can carry in your wallet. If the TBI patient is acting erratically or needs medical help, this card may help. It is available through: brainlaw.com

Appendix A

Victim Impact Statements

We had many community members or friends of the families write victim impact statements, here is an example of one from someone I don't know:

To whom it may concern.

As I type this, the thought comes to me. The "To Whom It May Concern" is all of us.

Because, the truth is, it does concern all of us. All the letters written for justice to be done, they are for each one of us. Anyone who has a family, anyone who is breathing at this very moment, we are the To Whom It May Concern.

Because it does concern us—that there could be even a remote chance that a person who has had such disregard for life, other than his own, would be allowed to serve anything but the mandatory sentence.

We, the To Whom It May Concern are asking for justice, for Abby and her family, and for all of us. That this person would not be free to ever inflict this kind of pain upon anyone again.

To truly see what was stolen—a life, and all the generations that would have come from that precious life. So much has been lost.

Time and memories that will not be able to happen—instead, a type of life sentence, if you will, for Abby's family and friends.

At Christmas, Thanksgiving, family functions, milestones, instead of the memories of a family, it's the constant knowing that their loved one was stolen from them, violently and suddenly without reason. No time to say good-bye. No time for a final hug and kiss.

Only the absolute rawness of a grief so deep and a pain so searing that there are no words to describe its depth— for it lives in a place words could not describe.

Is this about vengeance? Some may wrongly come to that conclusion.

But the truth is, no sentence could ever bring back the life and promise of Abby Davis. What we, The to Whom It May Concern, are asking is that your decision would truly be one that shows that you are concerned. Concerned about this scenario being replayed repeatedly in so many courtrooms across this Nation as we know that it is so very often . . .

It is Time now that we, The to Whom It May Concern, send a message that will resound not only in that courtroom, but across this Nation and for years to come that anything but the full extent of the law will ever be tolerated.

Help us to do that, please.

Time . . . The Davis Family did not lose that; it was stolen from them.

My Victim Impact Statement

When I asked the prosecutors how long I could talk, they said for as long as I wanted. Believe me I could talk for months about the effects this crash had on me, my family, our friends, and most important my daughter, but I want to make the most impact I can so after crying boatloads of tears, I will try to be short and to the point.

I am going to read this to help me get through it:

My life was perfect on Saturday May 13, 2017. It was my 56th birthday and our engagement party. Our friends hosted a party with about 40 people including our kids. Lexi brought her best friend Abby. There were lots of Hokies and Hokie families there; the girls spoke to many of them about how excited they were to become Hokies and the hope they had for their future. I flew to Dallas the following Tuesday to starting training for what was my dream job. That Tuesday I had lunch with my lifelong friend Julie who said to me that my life was perfect, and it was. Ray had now moved in with me; all four kids were in a great spot; Lexi, the baby, was getting ready to graduate high school and had finally chosen a college, Virginia Tech.

That Thursday, I received a text from Lexi with a photo showing her in bio lab dissecting a pig—the last photo I have of her before the crash. That Friday I was in training, meaning my phone was silenced, and saw I missed a call from Lexi's friend Brook. She never calls me. The message from Brook was: *Lexi and Abby had been hit by a large truck.*

My life will never be the same. When I finally reached Brooke, I spoke to Liz, a witness to the crash who is a nurse. She asked me if my daughter would have been the driver or the passenger in a blue CRV. I said it was Abby's car, so she should have been driving. She told me the driver didn't have a pulse and the passenger's pulse was very faint. I knew the passenger was being flown to the Level-1 trauma hospital, never a good sign. After frantically trying to get in touch with my son Marshall and Ray, my fiancé, I finally reached them. Marshall lives about five minutes from the hospital so he raced over and was the first to get there. I kept asking him to make sure it was Lexi who was there. Abby and Lexi looked a lot alike, long blonde hair, beautiful smiles that would light up any room, skinny and off the charts beautiful, although Abby was taller. You never want to have to tell your son to make sure the hospital does everything they can to keep his sister alive. No parent should ever have to do that. I finally caught a flight home from Dallas. I had to fly home not knowing when I landed if my daughter was alive or what I was walking into. It was eight hours after the crash that I reached the hospital. The anguish of being that far away was another layer of horror in this story.

My life completely froze for six weeks; my world became a small hospital room.

The day after the crash, Lexi was supposed to attend prom at another school. Back home I found her dress and jewelry laid out and a check list of things to do. Her senior prom was three weeks after the crash. We had been planning it for months, and she was excited. Instead of prom, there were memorial and other community events. Graduation was four weeks after the crash. Family was coming in from California and Utah. I had sent out her graduation announcements the Monday before the crash. All of that was snatched away from our entire family. Many, many things were stolen from us by a selfish individual who chose to do drugs and drink, and then drive on a beautiful Friday afternoon. High school graduation should have been a highlight of hundreds of 18-year-old's lives and their families—but was overlaid with sadness. My son had to accept his sister's diploma, and he looked so grief stricken. When she should have been graduating, I was standing outside while they changed my 18-year-old's diaper.

Lexi was in the burn trauma ICU for over two weeks. We didn't know what the extent of her brain injury would be until she woke up or if she would wake up. Her brain injury was the worst it could be—a diffuse anxioral injury with shearing. It was highly likely she would be in a vegetative state. The doctors didn't think she would make it through that first night. Your brain is what makes you who you are. Lexi was unconscious for two weeks; she didn't speak until June 9th. Once she was out of the coma, she wasn't sleeping more than 45 minutes a night, and would become very agitated, she would bite and hit and rock back and forth. It was a million times worse than anyone can imagine. When her brothers spent most of one day with her when she was in the step-down

unit at local trauma unit, they were both exhausted and said it was like taking care of a two-year-old.

My life is divided into before the crash and after the crash. I aged 20 years that first weekend. For the first eight months I would wake up every day and hope this was all a bad dream. Every day was very hard. The 19th of any month will never be the same. Lexi was in Atlanta at a traumatic brain injury rehabilitation hospital for over three months. We had 28 flights during that time with people flying in and out of Atlanta to take care of her, allowing my husband and me to keep our jobs. She was in incredible pain constantly for months and has had four surgeries. To watch your child in pain is excruciating for any loving parent. I would have given *anything to have been in the bed instead of her*. Our job as a parent is to protect our kids, and to have something like this happen is beyond any parent's worst nightmare. She had to relearn everything, like walking, swallowing, and eating.

(Referencing a photo in PowerPoint) Here is her arm in July 2017, when they couldn't find a vain to put in an IV, making it awful every time they poked and prodded her. At Shepherd Center inpatient they had to give her a shot in her stomach every night to prevent blood clots; her weight had dropped to 98 lbs., and she was skin and bones. We both cried and cried. She was in a wheelchair for months. She had to relearn how to walk, and in the middle of that, she broke her foot while at Shepherd Center. One of the worst days was when we had to tell her about Abby's death. We had to wait until she was keeping her short-term memories, which wasn't until July 27th. Hell doesn't begin to describe that experience. Look at all the photos (shown in PowerPoint) from Europe when Lexi and Abby were side by side. They pretty much stayed that way until the day

Abby was killed.

It was four months and two days from when she left to go to the beach until she walked back into our house. I had hoped it would be easier when she came home, but it wasn't. In addition to working full time, I had to coordinate doctor appointments, therapy, caregivers, and try to give her space to be "normal." One day we had 10 hours of appointments, until we both were beyond exhausted. I had to leave my dream job and go back to my previous industry because I was simply too stressed working nights and weekends.

I have been diagnosed with PTSD and have very bad anxiety, especially when driving or dealing with Lexi. Every time I hear a siren, I have a panic attack. Weird things will set me off, like last week when I made the same dinner I did the morning I left for Dallas, and a flood of memories came back to me and my heart raced, and I cried. When I hear of a traffic death, it literally takes my breath away like I have been punched in the stomach. I can be randomly driving or in a parking lot and when I see a Fly High Abby sticker, I will break down and sob. I couldn't deal with Abby's death for over six months. I still have a very hard time wrapping my head around it. I am terrified anytime I can't reach one of my kids or my husband. The few times Lexi has gone to the beach when she was home this summer, my anxiety is off the charts, especially if she doesn't text me back right away. I can't handle anything else happening to us; I feel it will literally kill me.

She is a miracle now, but I fought with every

fiber of my being to get her the best medical help. I pushed very hard to get her into Shepherd Center, one of the best brain injury rehab hospitals in the country. In addition to speech therapy, physical therapy, occupational and vision therapy that went on for seven months, we were able to provide hyperbaric chamber treatments, neurofeedback, and a specialized treatment for a week in Utah. Despite doing everything in my power, Lexi will never be the same as she was when she woke up on May 19, 2017.

She continues to have issues such as regulating her emotions, her body temperature is off, she is either hot or cold for no reason, she can't multi-task, if she is texting, there is no use talking to her because she can't listen. She loses things more often that an average person. She is in school, but it is much, much harder than it would have been before the crash. She needs special accommodations for college. It is very hard for her to be at Tech without Abby. When I am visiting Tech, Abby haunts me. Everywhere I go I think of Abby; here is where we took photos in the bookstore with Abby, etc. In addition to a severe brain injury Lexi has some vision loss. It is due to the optic nerve damage caused by the crash. As of right now, she will never be able to drive. Stop and think about that for a moment. She can't run to the store to pick up something, she will never be able to pick up her kids from school. When you must take a senior citizen's driver's license away from them, that is a pivotal moment in their life. Try that at 18 when you have your entire life in front of you. She had driven for almost exactly two years. What if you could never drive again? What is that worth to you? It is very hard on her but also on Ray and me as we need to drive her everywhere. With her vision issues, she must be very careful when she walks so she doesn't run into things. I am terrified she will be hit by a car while crossing the street. Once you have a brain injury, another bump to the head can be fatal. Even a minor injury could kill her. That is now what I must live with.

Her left arm is one of the most severe injuries many doctors around the country have ever seen. She was reaching back petting the puppy, Macy, when the crash happened. When she was stable enough to do surgery on June 1, the trauma doctor called me from the operating room and said, "Her arm was liquefied." He had been a trauma doctor for 30 years and had never fused anyone's elbow before. Her arm is now fixed at a 60-degree angle. It looks very natural in photos, but she can't straighten it or bend it. It doesn't move from that position. After much physical and occupational therapy, she can move her fingers, her wrist and her shoulder giving her some movement, but there are countless things she can't do. Her arm aches because her muscles want to be moved— even after 479 days it continues to bother her. We took her to the only doctor in the country at the Mayo clinic who thinks he can give her some movement. If she has the surgery, she will have some movement, but she has a 20 percent chance of being in constant pain. Also, the surgery would only last 5–7 years, and it would need to be re-done often. She had her fourth surgery last October to remove the pins and plates from her arm because the pins were about to poke through her skin.

Lexi was an athlete; she played field hockey; she swam on our neighborhood swim team; and she and I did yoga together. She was a lifeguard the summer of 2016 and was going to be a lifeguard supervisor in 2017. She loved being a lifeguard sitting in the sun and getting paid for it. She can never be a lifeguard again. She can't do any of that now, and never will be able to do anything that could cause injury to her head. She was at Hokie camp this summer at Virginia Tech, and I saw a video of other students crab-crawling, doing an obstacle course, and kayaking. When I asked her what she did during that time, she said, "I had to sit out." When I asked her if she felt awkward, she said, "Of course, Mom."

In addition to her physical issues, she has many emotional issues. I joke it is hard having a 19-year-old—then add a TBI, and it is impossible. She is very emotional, and I don't think she has dealt with Abby's death. I'm afraid she will have survivor's guilt the rest of her life. Of course, I am very worried about her self-medicating with drugs or alcohol, and her being depressed as well as the possibility of suicide. The risk of suicide in TBI patients is significantly higher, and that is without losing your best friend at the age of 18. She has horrible anxiety attacks where she gets flushed and can't breathe. It is awful to experience. She also gets dizzy easily, and the doctors think her blood pressure is not regulating correctly due to her brain injury. Here is a list of her medical conditions from her primary care doctor in August. If the Affordable Care Act (ACA) ever goes away so people with pre-existing conditions can't get insurance, she will be in a real mess. The morning she woke up on May 19 last year, she was perfectly healthy, now she is a "walking pre-exiting condition."

She had so many x-rays and CAT scans it was impossible to count, thus I worry about the long-term effects of those. In addition, studies have shown that TBI patients are at a 4.5 times greater risk for dementia and Alzheimer's.

This crash will haunt her for her entire life. Last Thursday she was hundreds of miles away at a recruiting event for a professional organization at Tech and was talking to a fellow student from Virginia Beach. When he found out where she was from, he asked her if she knew the girl who was killed in the crash near his house. She stood there and didn't know what to say. Later, she told him that it was her best friend who was killed in the crash, and she is the survivor. He took photos of her and sent out a group text to his friends. She just wants to be normal, and that isn't possible.

I have often wondered what if this had been a random accident? But it wasn't—this was 100 percent preventable. Doing drugs and drinking, and then driving are all 100 percent preventable. What I have shown you and told you doesn't begin to explain or express the agony and heartbreak this crash caused in our lives.

No one can understand what our family has been through. On the drive home from Hokie weekend in April of 2017, I told Abby and Lexi their future was so bright they both needed sunglasses. Abby's light was snuffed out.

In conclusion, Abby's life was cruelly taken away, we will never know how she could have improved the world, but for everyone who knew her, the world is not as bright. Lexi survived, but at a great cost. Every time Lexi opens her eyes, she only sees half the world, she can't straighten her arm or drive to her friend's house or participate in a million other activities that we all take for granted. When she graduates from Virginia Tech, Abby won't be there with her, like she should have been and they had planned. Abby's life was tragically cut short, and Lexi has a life sentence on so many, many levels.

Ray's Statement

I served 22 years in the United States Navy to support our constitution that gave the defendant the freedom to make choices. With this freedom he chose to consume alcohol, drugs and then to drive. Nobody forced him to do this. His choice plunged two families into a black hole of pain and sorrow that no family should ever experience.

Any journey that involves repeated trauma of whatever sort is essentially private. No one else can truly know what it's like, and what you go through. Nor would they want to, because to really know it is to experience all the pain and fear and exhaustion, the ugly and difficult moments, and the darkness when you're not sure light will ever return.

I never knew I had so many tears. I can't explain the exhaustion, the feeling of helplessness, the anger, and the injustice I felt. I wanted to hurt the person that put us in this black hole from a choice he made. Doesn't matter how fine a son, brother, uncle or husband he is. He made a choice, and we suffered the consequences.

My wife and I didn't sleep much during this period, and our sleep patterns have never corrected themselves. Gone was my wife's infectious laughter, and now she is much more guarded. For over three months, we rarely saw each other while we rotated weeks in Atlanta at the rehab center.

Trying to work during this period was extremely difficult. When I was at work, I felt guilty for not being by my daughter's side. When I was in Atlanta, I missed my wife as she was home trying to work.

This journey hasn't and will never end. Our daughter has lifelong injuries that can never be corrected. Our fear is constant and never-ending. If she suffers another concussion, chances are she will never recover.

All this pain, sorrow, exhaustion, and fear was inflicted by a choice.

Appendix B

Helpful "Self-Talk"

This is a list of some self-talk that helped me through the dark days:

- This too shall pass, and my life will be better.

- I am doing the best I can, given my history and level of current awareness.

- Like everyone else, I am a fallible person and at times will make mistakes and learn from them.

- There are no failures, only different degrees of success.

- Be honest and true to myself.

- It is okay to let myself be distressed for a while.

- I am not helpless. I can and will take the steps needed to get through this crisis.

- I will remain engaged and involved instead of isolating and withdrawing during this situation.

- One step at a time.

- I know I will be okay no matter what happens.

- Don't sweat the small stuff—it's all small stuff.

- There is less stress in being optimistic and choosing to be in control.

- I will do whatever is necessary to make tomorrow better.

Wisdom to Impart: What You Need to Know Right Away in the Event of Severe Trauma

This is my personal list of things that helped me get through each day:

- ✓ Get your loved one to the best hospital. If he or she isn't taken there right away, get them transferred. We know of someone who was in a bad car accident with a traumatic brain injury and she wasn't at a trauma center. She has on-going issues because her care wasn't the best.

- ✓ Someone needs to be the patient's advocate. If you can't speak up and be forceful, then assign someone else. When Lexi had trouble sleeping and then had finally fallen asleep, I sat outside her door and wouldn't let anyone go in and wake her up to take her vitals. I was the Mama Bear.

- ✓ The hospital will keep waking the patient up at all hours of the day and night. To stop this, ask for a "do not disturb" order so your loved one can sleep through the night.

- ✓ Get to the best rehab hospital you can. Again, you may have to fight and do some research, but it will be worth it.

- ✓ Your first shot at recovery is your best shot.

- ✓ If someone you love is in an accident, it may be hours before the police contact you.

- ✓ Take notes because you will need them later.

- ✓ Be kind to everyone, especially the nurses. They are the true angels of the ICU. We kept bringing them food as it was the only way we could thank them at that time.

✓ You will meet many wonderful people along the way. Get their contact information so you can keep in touch. Most people don't know what you have been through; however, these people do.

✓ If the person is over 18, apply for Social Security Disability and Medicaid right away. Even if you have insurance, not everything will be covered, and you will have co-pays that a second insurance will help cover. The hospital should have someone to help you. This was a godsend to me. It took over six months for everything to get approved—and I never would have thought of this. Plus, there are tons of things you need to provide, and they can help guide you. I also needed the reminders they sent me.

✓ Don't Google or research anything about the diagnosis. As much as I feel information is power, I was too overwhelmed to do this. However, other families have told me they did—and it was awful. In this case ignorance is bliss. You might want to have a trusted friend or family member find out the best treatments and hospitals for you.

✓ A traumatic brain injury is a marathon, not a sprint.

✓ Every brain injury is unique, so don't go by what you hear from others, but get the best help you can for your loved one.

✓ Try to be there for the doctor's rounds. Ask the nurses when rounds are. This is your chance to find out exactly what is going on, and be prepared to ask lots of questions. This is the only time you see the lead doctor.

✓ Stimulate the patient while he or she is in a coma. Read books, bring things in that smell, and be sure to massage and talk to them. It can't hurt. Once the patient wakes up, keep up the stimulation, but be sure to have significant quiet time. Follow the schedule the hospital gives you.

✓ Watch what you talk about even before your loved one regains consciousness. When my son and I were talking about the accident, a tear rolled down Lexi's face.

✓ Use all connections you have; people want to help and often can. When Lexi's surgery kept getting pushed back, I contacted a friend who contacted the president of the hospital and her surgery happened the next day. Coincidence? Maybe, but maybe not . . .

✓ They told us the first six months she would make the most improvement, then the next year to year-and-a-half she would continue. Never give up. I spoke to someone who was eight years out from his injury, and he progressed the most in year seven.

✓ You will be overwhelmed by all the paperwork. Keep it all and create a binder or boxes with the various sections: insurance, Social Security, doctor's contacts, etc. This may be something you can ask a family member or close friend to organize for you.

✓ When someone asks if they can help you, give them a task to do and say thank you. It will make your life easier, and they really want to help.

✓ Post-Traumatic Stress Disorder (PTSD) is real. You will all need help to recover. Get the help you need.

Hopefully, things will improve, and you will survive this horrible time. Hold on to hope.

How Debbie wishes she didn't have this story to tell. Debbie lives in Virginia with her amazing husband, Ray. Debbie is an award-winning salesperson and since May 2017 has become an advocate for anyone suffering a brain injury. Through her writing and speaking, she hopes to help bring awareness to the challenges of traumatic brain injury and caregiving.

Her most important jobs are being a mom to her children and Yaya to her two beautiful grandchildren.

Email Debbie at: debbie@youcantimaginebook.com

Follow her on her website: youcantimaginebook.com

www.ingramcontent.com/pod-product-compliance
Lightning Source LLC
Chambersburg PA
CBHW051551030726

47592CB00001B/237